A FAIR COP

By
MAUREEN INGRAM SCOTT

Printed by Clydeside Press
ISBN 1 873586 07 8

With sincere thanks to Eileen

Dedicated to all police officers.

Past, present and future

CHAPTER ONE

THE BEGINNING

It was 10.30p.m. A cold, wet, raw night. We picked our way through the stinking debris of empty fish boxes that littered the pavements and gutters of the Bridgegate. In the dim light, a rat darted across our path in search of some rotten discarded morsel.

He cursed, "so, how long have you been in the job?"

"Four nights."

Rain dripped from the overhead railway bridge.

He shook his head "four nights".

I tried to catch a glimpse of the face hidden below the shadow of the slashed peak of his hat "and you?"

"30 years. This is my last night. I'm not sorry. I won't miss it ...The best of luck to you…..T.J.F.

And with that he was gone through the archway, and I never saw him again…..

CHAPTER TWO

DECISION TIME

I was fifteen years old and a decision had to be made. When the careers officer informed me that higher education was not necessary to join the police, I immediately left school, much to the disappointment and annoyance of my parents.

At my mum's insistence, I embarked on a shorthand-typing course followed by work in a solicitor's office. I found being tied to a desk extremely monotonous but Miss Smith, my very understanding boss frequently devised ploys, which allowed me some freedom.

A few years later, financial gain caused me to change jobs and I bore the brunt of a humourless head lady's inexplicable hatred of new employees. Wastebaskets were examined each day, resulting in the purchase of a large bag into which I secretly placed my frequent faux pas. My only ray of sunshine was the mounted police-man who spotted me at my little window and we would exchange a wave.

At home, the subject of the police was never discussed, but on reaching the joining age of twenty, I confided in my dad who accompanied me to Police Headquarters, a grey, imposing building in St Andrews Street, Glasgow. The sergeant's words echoed in my head. I was 5'5" and the minimum height was 5'5 **and one half inch**. We drove home in silence as I fought back the tears.

Some time later, I learned of a west end clinic which specialised in stretching people and after a short course at an address of which I have no recollection, I was once again slipping out of my shoes and stepping forward to the measuring stick. I took a deep breath and could feel the protruding guage brushing my head. "I'm touching it," I hissed through clenched teeth, my lungs bursting. There was not a happier person in the world when the Sergeant handed over the elusive application form.

I was not prepared, however, for the reaction of my mum. She stood silently in front of the cooker, tears rolling down her cheeks, as she stared and stirred at the contents of a pot. Her only child, from a quiet residential area, joining the police. My dad was told in no uncertain terms if anything happened to me, she would never forgive him. She would not look at the application form, preferring to ignore its existence.

I remember little of the educational examination except the piece of literature dictated to us by a very helpful highland Sergeant who pro noun ced ev er y syl la ble.

I do remember, however, the medical examination. A most embarrassing experience as I walked the length of the room half naked, feeling that I was being scrutinised for some purpose far removed from police work.

Only the interview with the policewoman Superintendent remained. Mrs Beattie was very interested in my hobby of amateur dramatics and went on at great lengths about Shakespeare and the Citizens Theatre. I felt rather nervous informing her that my interest was limited to Church plays. Nevertheless I was accepted. I was ecstatic, my dad was secretly delighted and my mum heartbroken. The partners in my office were surprised and the head lady furious that after all her training she would have to re-train a new start. I didn't care.

At last I was going to be a policewoman in the City of Glasgow Police.

CHAPTER THREE

TRAINING CENTRE

I stood proudly in uniform admiring myself from every angle in the mirror at home, but the next morning as I sat on the bus on my way to the Training Centre in Oxford Street, I was absolutely terrified that a member of the public would be silly enough to place their particular problem in my incapable hands.

Oxford Street was a large building on the south side of the River Clyde with several classrooms. It also housed Gorbals Police Office; a section house for single and visiting policemen, and a small canteen which I am certain has never appeared in any good food guide. There was never a very wide selection. If you were reasonably early you could choose a dish which you knew from past experience wasn't too bad, but if you were late, all that was left were the dishes everyone knew to avoid, and if you were really late it was soup, rubbery, raspberry jelly with a small wrapped block of ice cream, coffee and on a lucky day a chocolate biscuit. There was also a small quadrangle doubling as a car park and parade ground.

During the two week course, the Sergeant, God, to us raw recruits, took us to the Glasgow District Court at St. Andrews Street where we were officially sworn in as police officers and supplied with a voluminous City of Glasgow Police Instruction Book which amongst other things under the Glasgow Bye Laws made it an offence to jump the queue in a car at the Renfrew Ferry, or to beat a carpet outwith certain hours, and a lady was not allowed to clean windows in excess of 22'.

We were instructed in the art of marching which posed no problem for the majority but unfortunately one member of the class was totally uncoordinated and led with left arm and leg much to the consternation of those behind.

A parade inspection would follow and while being complimented on my bulled shoes, my shirt collar always attracted the Inspector's attention. He would place his two fingers in the offending space between throat and collar and order my return to the clothing store, refusing to accept that my neck appeared to defy anything in stock.

Although my memory of those days has faded, one remains vivid. The instructor had arranged a visit to the City Mortuary for those of us who had never seen a dead body. Three of us called at the inconspicuous brick building in Saltmarket. "Just come through" smiled the beady-eyed man, his shoulders hunched as he rubbed his hands together. "I don't think I've any interesting ones". I am certain it had nothing to do with being courteous that prompted my two colleagues to usher me to the front. There was an indescribable odour in the cold, white, tiled room, its sparseness broken only by two porcelain slabs in the centre. The attendant's voice echoed and hissed as he whispered respectfully "come closer". We shuffled forward. "Closer". Hesitantly we moved a few inches nearer a drawer in the wall, which he opened slowly, exposing the purple, bloated body of a drowned man. In the long silence that followed, I wondered if my fellow officers could hear the pounding of my heart as I averted my gaze to the ceiling, inwardly pleading with

God not to let me faint.   I felt the chill in my body being quickly replaced by a sudden wave of heat, but at that moment the drawer closed and another opened to reveal a very peaceful looking, elderly lady, the only indication of death being the unmistakable pallor.   The doll like features of a stillborn baby concluded our visit and we declined the offer of a cup of tea.

Stepping outside we were very conscious of the traffic noise in contrast to the eerie silence within the building and involuntarily gasped in deep breaths of fresh air. Suddenly there was a loud screech of brakes, two bangs and the sound of broken glass.   Our visit to the Mortuary was forgotten as we quickly recalled our classroom lecture for a road accident report.   Fortunately there were no injuries and little damage to the three vehicles involved.   I opened my new, unused notebook ... "Name?, age?, date of birth?, address?, occupation?"   I glanced at the tall man by my side as he slowly replied "police officer – on holiday.   Is this your first accident report?"   I nodded.   He then proceeded to provide all the necessary details and after a quick consultation with my two colleagues to make sure they had followed the correct procedure, the three drivers continued on their way leaving only a few bits of glass lying at the kerbside as evidence of their momentary lapse of concentration. Back at the training school, after explaining why we were late, the Sergeant decided to use our accident as a class exercise and was very impressed that we had coped so well until he learned the occupation of my driver.

Soon our two weeks ended and we were ready for the next stage of our training.

CHAPTER FOUR

TULLIALLAN FIRST STAGE

The initial or first stage training at Tulliallan Police College lasted for four weeks. Never a great scholar, I enjoyed college life, but found memorising and understanding all the various aspects of police work quite daunting. We quickly realised that the Sergeants at Oxford Street had not been Gods because the ones at Tulliallan certainly were. We studied Scottish Criminal Law from another voluminous loose leafed book commonly referred to for some reason as the Aberdeen Manual.

Numerous practical exercises formed part of our training and on one occasion I was partnered with a tall, heavily built highland student. The scene was a park which we were patrolling when directed by a member of the public to a body lying on the grass (both ably acted by members of the class). As we approached the inert figure, Archie announced in his soft, lilting accent, "I will organise the ambulance". He then shot off at great speed until halted by the instructor who told him to assume that an ambulance had been summoned and to proceed with the exercise.

At this time, policewomen were given separate additional instruction in dealing with crimes of a sexual nature involving females and children. I realise now how much times have changed as my mum's reaction when I told her of my tuition was "oh well, you'll know it all now. You won't need me to tell you anything". I was 21 years old.

P.T. and swimming were a welcome break from our academic studies even though the three-mile runs through the college grounds were pretty arduous. The method of determining swimmers and non-swimmers was rather unique. Those who dived or jumped from the top diving board and swam the length of the pool were swimmers, those who reneged were non-swimmers. I could swim a length of the pool but was unsure of jumping in from such a height. Each step to the top diving board became a test in itself. After what seemed an eternity I was standing with a few others shouting encouragement to the unfortunate student edging his way along the narrow strip of wood. All too soon it was my turn. The instructor's whistle sounded and he bellowed out "next". As I stood teetering on the edge I could hear his voice "look straight ahead, think positive, go, go, go, don't look down", but I had looked down and the sight of my fellow officers like pin pricks on a sheet of paper determined my category. I nervously retraced my steps. "Non swimmer Miss Ingram" he shouted in his east coast accent noting the fact on a clipboard. "Next".

Although the occasional romance flourished, intensive study precluded it. I did however "fall" for one policeman who appeared totally unaware of my feelings. John was a Catholic and this inspired one of my friends to give me a blue St. Christopher which looked like the Virgin Mary. Quite why Pat thought that divine intervention might help I don't know and it didn't. Although my little blue St. Christopher on its silver chain conspicuously adorned my neck day and night, John did not notice me and with his David Essex black curly hair and blue eyes I did not have the courage to make my feelings known.   I heard much later that John had left the police, deciding that it was not the job for him.

The four weeks ended. Marching and inspections were somewhat mundane now and we were reasonably adept at parade ground synchronised traffic signals.   We returned for a final week to the Glasgow Training School at Oxford Street.

CHAPTER FIVE

OXFORD STREET RE-VISITED

It was during this final week of our initial training that the male officers were allocated a division. Policewomen did not perform beat duties along with male colleagues. We were attached to the policewomen's department situated within the Central Division, then located in Turnbull Street. In charge was a policewoman Superintendent – Mrs Beattie. We were commonly referred to as Mrs Beattie's girls. She spoke with a polite accent and had lowered her voice a few octaves for effect. There were two shifts – A and B and I became an A shift girl.

On our last Thursday, all students reported to their respective divisions at 7.00 pm and worked with a senior Constable for three hours.

I was neighboured to June, a very pleasant girl. At 5'9" she felt very conspicuous alongside my 5'5" and insisted on walking along the gutters while I walked on the pavement. During our patrol, a flashing light summoned us to the red police box and I felt rather important entering for the first time this hallowed sanctuary seldom seen by law abiding citizens. The basic interior comprised a wooden bench with high stool and a 'phone from which we took a report of a stolen motor vehicle entering it in our notebooks and in a rather shoddy hard back book which lay on the chipped, well worn work top, to be read by the beat man for the area when he next called at the box. An ill fitting drawer contained an untidy selection of forms to cover every eventuality requiring a report and a bare light bulb hung precariously on a dirty wire, highlighting cobwebs and grimy roof. The only creature comfort was a wall heater beneath the desk. Later we attended an alarm bell ringing at a shop in Buchanan Street. Having made sure that there were no obvious signs of a break-in, we waited until the keyholder came and, armed with my new black rubber torch (policewomen were not issued with batons) we searched the premises. Secretly I was relieved when it proved to be a false alarm.

A cup of tea back at the office and a friendly chat with some of the girls ended my first evening patrolling the streets of Glasgow.

In class the next day we all had stories to relate and at the end of our final day, as we all went our separate ways, felt a mixture of excitement and apprehension. We still had a long way to go in our two year probationary period and at any time could be told what was termed "unlikely to become" (a suitable police officer), and asked to resign.

CHAPTER SIX

THE POLICEWOMEN'S DEPARTMENT

The policewomen's department was on the second floor of the old building.   Mrs Beattie's room was on one side of the landing and the Chief Inspector and Inspectors had a small room on the other side.   A large room next door was the hub of our activities.   At one end was a large dining table and in the corner a Belling cooker with two rings, an oven and an instruction on the wall advising that only two rings or one ring and the oven could be operated at one time.   In the middle was an assortment of desks with lockers along one side and small windows along the other side.   At the opposite end of the room was another table at which the Sergeant and/or shift Inspector sat.   Above her head was a shelf with three box files, two containing current indecency reports and one containing shoplifting reports.   During quiet periods, we were expected to read the contents of the aforementioned files.   However, due to a reluctance to be seen perusing the indecency files, new policewomen found themselves more adept in the preparation of shoplifting cases.

Initially, due to a lack of confidence in my ability to deal with any incoming enquiries, I attempted to avoid answering the telephone, but this was quickly noticed by our Inspector who instructed me to answer all calls.

Being an old building, the lift was very temperamental and on one occasion broke down between floors with someone inside.   Hearing the poor unfortunate shouting for help had alerted assistance, but a few of us gathered on our landing shouting "helpful comments!!" until we were told it was Mrs Beattie, minus her usual contralto tones.   We quickly scattered.

Our shifts were more extensive than our male counter-parts although we worked slightly shorter hours.

7.00 am to 2.00 pm was either a patrol shift or blind escort.   On an early patrol it was routine to look in at the Central Station and St Enoch Station toilets, and chats with the lady attendants often resulted in missing girls being picked up.   A visit to the Salvation Army Hostel was also fruitful on many occasions.   We often called at the women's hostel in Carrick Street.   I recall the warm atmosphere of the place being provided by a long furnace like fire which extended along the room and the peculiar and unpleasant odour I attributed to the socks and other various items of clothing draped over it. Although all offers of cups of tea and rolled up ciggies were politely refused, the heat was most welcome on a freezing cold or wet day.

"Dosses" were a very important feature on an early shift. A place where on a cold and wet morning a hot cup of coffee and a bacon roll was especially welcome.   One such place was the British European Airways terminal in St Enoch Square, but more popular was a café in a lane running from the Fishmarket down to the Clyde side.   It had the advantage of having two exits.   Some of the worthies would alert us if the Sergeant was approaching giving us time to escape by the other door.   Of course the Sergeant was well aware of this dodge as she had practised it many times on her patrol days but the report of her presence in the area had the desired effect of getting us back out on the street.

On patrol with Doris one morning she spotted a young man approaching with his fly undone. "Right Maureen, you deal with this" she instructed me in her Kelvinside accent. Horrified, I took a deep breath "Excuse me sir, uhm, you're not dressed". He stood, a puzzled expression on his face "I'm sorry". I cleared my throat and nodding towards the offending area, tried again "you're not decent". He gazed at me in total confusion until Doris took command of the situation "your fly is undone sir". In a quick "flash" and slight bend of the knees the wayward zip had been returned to its correct position, and he continued on his way with a quick thanks and bemused smile leaving behind one very embarrassed brand new policewoman.

I enjoyed doing the blind escort. We would meet the ladies and gentlemen alighting from buses in Hope Street and escort them across busy Sauchiehall Street to Renfrew Street where they would board another bus which took them to the Blind Craft Centre. They were always cheerful and chatty. As we waited to cross the road, Andy would tell you "that car's miles away dear, c'mon, we've got loads of time".

One sad incident has remained etched in my memory. While on patrol, a lady rushed up to tell us that a man had collapsed in the street. He died on his way to hospital. From the papers in his wallet we found out that he lived on the south side of Glasgow. There was no-one in, but a neighbour told us that his wife worked in an office not far from where he had taken ill. It turned out that he had been en route to meet her. There is no format laid down in any instruction book as to how to break the news of the death of a loved one. You just try to be as gentle, sympathetic, and helpful as you possibly can. After identifying her husband, a police driver drove us to her home.   During the journey she spoke of nursing her elderly mother and it was only on the recent death of her mother that she and her husband had married. We left her in the care of a good friend and neighbour. Years later I spoke with a male colleague who told me he had been the driver that day and had been moved by my sympathetic handling of the situation.   I only hope the lady thought so too.

Points duty was a terrifying ordeal. As I stepped out into the middle of the junction of Stockwell Street and Howard Street under the watchful eye of Anne, a girl with a vast four years experience, cars, vans and lorries seemed to pass at amazing speeds on either side of me.   Initially, it was difficult to decide which car to stop, and then when I had my right arm straight up to stop oncoming traffic and my left arm out to the side to stop traffic behind me, my mind became a complete blank as to how to instruct the traffic to the right and left of me to proceed.   I eventually solved this by nodding my head to the left then to the right.   Fortunately all the drivers appeared to understand this unusual signal and later Anne reminded me of my Tulliallan lessons.

I also had an embarrassing time at Charlotte Street pedestrian crossing.   A local worthy best described as "not the full shilling" took a "fancy" for me.   He would appear at the side of the crossing with his bagpipes. Dressed in an ill fitting kilt and jacket, he would play a barely recognisable Scotland the Brave.   As I stepped out on to the crossing to allow the schoolchildren to cross, I found it almost impossible not to keep step.   My suggestion that he walk into the city centre met with a wide toothy grin and an insistence that he would rather keep me company.

It was always necessary to have a quick reply for the "know alls" and no-one could do it better than Doris who on one occasion had a young driver cringing so much with embarrassment he was almost wedged between his brake and accelerator pedals.   She was directing traffic at St Enoch Square when a young man approached in a very flashy sports car, hood down, sunglasses on, and radio blasting out the hits of the day.   Not realising that Doris was holding up the traffic to allow pedestrians to cross, he blasted continuously on his two tone horn to the drivers in front.   Very slowly Doris walked back to his car.   A long manicured nail pointing to the radio required no further instruction.   Putting on her haughtiest expression she diverted her gaze back to him "and what else did mummy give you for your birthday?"   He attempted to explain that he had not seen her but Doris continued her onslaught.   "At great expense I have been kitted out in this hideous, oversized, ankle length dirty white coat.   I find it frightening to learn that you didn't see me".   Slowly retracing her steps to her point with its bemused onlookers, she saved him further embarrassment by waving on the traffic.

CHAPTER SEVEN

PARKING DUTY

Parking duty could be either 8.00am to 3.00pm or 11.00am to 6.00pm.   It was hated by most people, although some men did it permanently as it was a constant day shift.   Duty began in the muster hall at Central Division when stolen car registration numbers and any other relevant information was read out and noted.   Forms for the previous day's bookings were also completed.   One morning I was approached by a policeman with a tale of woe regarding his friend whom I had booked the previous day.   After consultation with my neighbour we agreed to discard it (an impossible action now).   The next morning the policeman told me his friend had been really grateful.   He placed an envelope in my hand which his friend had given him adding that he didn't know if I smoked or not.   When I opened the envelope in my neighbour's presence she whispered "give it back to him", not wanting even to touch the offending £1 note we were gazing at.   I was also horrified especially when the policeman wouldn't take it back, and it was only when he witnessed me putting it in the office charity box and promised to tell his friend, that my neighbour and I breathed a sigh of relief.

I developed my own system for booking drivers which I felt was quite fair.   If the vehicle was very modern and/or company owned, I booked the driver, but if the vehicle was a bit run down and had the obvious signs of being a family car, I dismissed the driver with a warning.   This kept my number of bookings up but didn't hurt people like my dad who could ill afford a parking fine.

The police box in St Enoch Square was a central meeting point before taking up your allocated area for parking duty. Many times we were asked by curious bystanders if there were stairs to an office below. There weren't. The girls sat on the high counter and the men huddled around. It was an eerie sight on a wet day when the heater caused steam to rise from soggy raincoats.

In St Enoch Square, the majority of those parking cars were reps. from the local offices. There was a good rapport and we could allow vehicles to block each other knowing where we could contact their owners. I often looked up at my office window remembering the mounted policeman's friendly smile, and even on the wettest day I never regretted my decision to join the police. By the time winter came along I was the proud owner of a very expensive pair of almost new, ankle length fur lined boots, courtesy of a stupid ruling whereby policewomen who married were compelled to leave the job. (In 1968 this ruling was abolished). Many excellent, experienced girls were lost in this way, but although Marion could no longer "walk the streets", her boots did for a good few years.

On one of those miserable wintry days I was suffering from a combination of a bad cold and "that time of the month". The elderly beat man commented to my neighbour that I wasn't my usual cheery self and she quietly explained the reason. Gently he took me by the arm "right lass, you come with me. I know just the thing for you". Meekly I followed him into a nearby building where he sat me down in a warm office by the entrance. "The lass isn't feeling too good" he whispered to the doorman who disappeared for a few moments returning with a glass of clear liquid. "You get that down you. It will do you good". I was in no mood to argue or enquire as to the contents and, fearful of the taste, did as I was told and downed the fluid in one large gulp. As the two astonished men gazed at me, I gasped as I felt a burning sensation travel down the full length of my frozen body. When I recovered sufficiently to manage an intake of breath, the policeman smiled "well lass, I didn't expect you to take it as quickly as that". "What is it?" I wheezed. They both laughed "you're in a Bond and that was 100 proof whisky". To this day I don't know if it cured me or I was just oblivious to everything, but somehow I reached the end of my shift.

A particular van driver caused my neighbour and I some consternation. Between 8.00am and 9.30am. there was a no loading and unloading ban on most of the city centre's main streets. The cheeky lad would wait until we walked to the bottom of Stockwell Street. He would then drive quickly up to the shop premises he was delivering to at the other end of Stockwell Street, carry out his delivery and drive off before we could reach him. Several warnings to the shopkeeper proved useless. One morning we arranged for the motor cyclists to remain out of sight in Howard Street. As we approached Clyde Street, on cue the van shot past us and made its usual stop. We signalled our motor cyclists – a fair cop I think.

In winter, our uniforms definitely came under the category, quantity rather than quality. We wore vest, shirt, pullover, jacket, lining, thick tights, trousers, boots (only ankle length allowed), two individual waterproof leggings with straps which fastened on to the buttons of your jacket pocket, raincoat and finally a hat cover which extended down over the raincoat collar. Some girls wore paper collars (all collars were detachable), but on a wet day these would slowly disintegrate leaving a red raw line around the neck.

One memory still makes me smile.   A group of us en route to St Enoch Square box boarded a bus at Glasgow Cross.   As we climbed the stairs, one of Ella's leggings began to trail behind her. Unbuttoning her raincoat and lining, she discovered that her uniform pocket button had come adrift. Someone suggested that she fasten the legging on to her breast pocket button, which she did.   All was well until she tried to stand up.   There was no quick way of correcting her abnormality with the result she had to quasi modo from the bus to St Enoch police box, receiving a few strange looks along the way.

None of us liked going to be measured for our uniforms and we always went in pairs as one of the tailors seemed to enjoy his work just a little too much.   They never fitted anyway.   The usual practice was to keep the bits that weren't too bad and exchange the rest between ourselves.

About this time my dad discovered that helping me to join the police did not afford him special privileges.   He was driving me into the policewomen's department en route to his own work when his car was involved in a very minor bump. I asked him for details of his insurance etc. "I'll give them to you tonight, I'll be late for work" he smiled, but much to his consternation Miss Bossy Boots in uniform insisted.   I never admitted to him that I later realised I needn't have been involved if he and the other driver were quite happy to exchange particulars. That night as he complained to my mum, she raised her hand "don't expect my sympathy, you're the one who encouraged her". By this time my mum had accepted my career and although I don't think she ever stopped worrying about me, she never mentioned it.

As Christmas approached, so did pedestrian control. A horrible unappreciated duty whereby our outstretched arms at traffic lights were meant to prevent hordes of Christmas shoppers crossing when the "little red man" was illuminated.

Three young men decided to ignore my efforts and began to dodge between the moving traffic. I stopped them on the opposite pavement. Two listened very patiently to my lecture and apologised, but the third began to walk away. A male colleague appeared to lend his support and stood patiently as I charged the youth with jaywalking and demanded his name and address. – "51 Collier Street" he replied confidently. I then allowed him to join his friends. I felt I had dealt with the situation quite competently until I returned to the office and could find no trace of Collier Street in the street directory. "Where did this take place?" enquired one of the girls. "Outside Arnott Simpsons".

They looked at each other and began to laugh. "Do you know what shop is opposite?"

As I shook my head they burst into song "John Collier, John Collier, the window to watch". (A well known T.V. advertisement of the day for a gent's outfitters).

On Christmas Eve I was directing traffic at Argyle Street/Miller Street, in place of the regular points man who was ill. As I stood in the rain in my massive raincoat, a van stopped.

"Where's big John?"

"Off sick".

"You'd better have this then"

and off he drove. Packages of varying shapes, sizes and smells followed, plus a handful of sweets and other goodies. I ended that day with fish, sausages, daily newspapers, sweets and chocolate biscuits.

The Christmas party was great fun when our Chief Inspector, Inspector, and Sergeants proved that they could enjoy themselves just as much as us. It was presided over by Mrs Beattie, the Superintendent. The Inspectors sang "I want an old fashioned house (an Eartha Kitt song) emphasizing the last line "and an old fashioned millionaire. I had an "L" sign pinned on me and was dressed in June's (5' 9") uniform and she in mine to illustrate our ill fitting uniforms which prompted Mrs Beattie's comment "who is that? Is she one of ours?"

CHAPTER EIGHT

SETTLING IN

I found as time went on that due to shifts I began to lose touch with many school friends and my social life and friends began to centre around the policewomen's department.   The toilet on the half landing was a great meeting place, out with the gaze or earshot of the Inspector or Sergeants, where nights out, boyfriends, and new eligible policemen could be discussed.   We had a very good system of vetting.   In each division there was a file containing the particulars of policemen in that division. A 'phone call to the divisional policewomen quickly ascertained their marital status.   I was asked out by an officer in the Southern Division, the proud owner of an old but immaculate Jaguar, who stayed in the police barracks in Merrylee Road.   The check revealed that he was the divisional gigolo but single.   On our third date he invited me back to his room.   As he opened his bedroom door, a blast of hot air hit me.   He left me there and returned a short while later with piping hot coffee.   As we sat chatting, he casually enquired if I was feeling it warm.   When I confessed that I was, he suggested that perhaps I would be more comfortable if I took off my dress.   When I suggested that perhaps he could open a window instead, he proceeded to lecture me on how, on each date a girl should give in a little more.   Obviously the third date was what we policewomen called "crunch time".   I can disclose that I was not in the Jaguar or the furnace again.

As in every job, the police had its share of flesh creepers. One such Sergeant would feel the ear lobe of an unsuspecting new policewoman and take great delight in announcing loudly "you had a sexy time last night. I can always tell". Any blushes of course added to his perverse pleasure. Today this behaviour would not be tolerated, but then it was in our half landing conference room that new recruits were warned.

I became particularly friendly with Maggie who had a few months more service than me. She was a complete extrovert with a pale face, huge brown eyes and long black hair which she could expertly coil and secure so that not one strand strayed on to her collar, a heinous crime which would provoke a reprimand by an astute Inspector. She was extremely intelligent, a conclusion I reached while listening to her answering most of the questions on University Challenge one night. While I sat and pretended I didn't want to play, Maggie complained about the silly questions. I was very grateful we did not go to Police College together. She would telephone me from there complaining bitterly that her classmates were so boring as they studied all evening, something she didn't have to do.

Duty at the High Court resulted in Maggie dramatically declaring her undying love for Jimmy Boyle who could not possibly be guilty of anything as he was far too good looking !!

She discovered a very dirty, scabby looking, pregnant black moggie crawling from the Central Police Office coal cellar. For the remainder of that day while carrying out our various duties, we coerced every police officer we met into subscribing to our cat kitty. We then arranged for her to be housed at the hospital of the vet who attended the police dogs and horses. When he heard our story he treated her eye infection, cleaned out her coal dust blocked ears, applied some beauty treatment on her matted fur and generally gave her some well needed T.L.C. In the meantime we had coaxed and cajoled the police janitor who in turn coaxed and cajoled his wife, into adopting her. The conclusion was that she became a much loved, cared for cat with enough tins of food to stock a shop, as the vet wouldn't accept payment and it was the only thing we could think of to spend the money on.

One Detective Inspector until the day he retired, used the story to his advantage. He was known for his meanness, but would call on me to verify that he couldn't be mean because when he was a Detective Constable he had contributed to the cat kitty.

Later in our service, Maggie and I were quite often chosen for plain clothes duties, more of which I shall write later. We worked well together in plain clothes, but unfortunately Maggie became another victim of the "no married policewomen" policy.

CHAPTER NINE

COURT DUTY

A 9.00 am/4.00 pm court duty at the Stipendiary Magistrate's court in Turnbull Street was usually quite a source of amusement with its regular clientele of misfits. It was a large imposing barren place devoid of any decoration, with tiered wooden benches.   It did, however, have one attractive feature.   It was warm and was therefore a sanctuary for some of life's pathetic souls who would sit quietly, anxious that any behaviour attracting attention would result in them all being ejected from the court.

Annie was one such person – a pleasant wee wumman when sober but absolutely obnoxious in drink.   The Central cells, where many spent the night before appearing at court the following morning were very basic.   The floor was concrete and the bed was a slightly raised area of concrete on to which was placed a mattress and blanket supplied at the time of incarceration.   A white porcelain toilet without seat reposed in the corner and was flushed from outside the cell.   Annie, on entering the cell, would immediately strip, accompanying this with a tirade of abuse, and in the morning would sit with her blanket around her, refusing to dress.   On a freezing wintry night, Annie encountered the Central Division's most formidable female attendant, known as turnkeys.   She ordered Annie to dress herself.   "Fuck off" came the reply.   The turnkey repeated the request with the same result.   She then removed all Annie's clothing, mattress and blanket.   Sev-

eral times during that night, Annie's plaintive wails could
be heard "gie's ma claithes. It's no fer. Ahm freezing.
Ma arse is stuck tae the cludgie". By morning she was
desperate to get dressed and from that day, on her frequent overnight visits, she was never a problem.

Another well known trouble maker could not believe his
luck when granted his request for a cigarette and match,
but he quickly reverted to form when he discovered it was
a safety match.

Law abiding citizens through drink can sometimes find
themselves in embarrassing situations. A young company
director after a very enjoyable night out, felt that the taxi
driver was taking him a long route home. He remon-
strated with the driver who stopped and ordered him out
of the taxi. He refused and next found himself at a police
office being given the opportunity of paying his fare, which
he again refused to do. Sitting in a cell on an old foam
mattress with a blanket but minus trouser belt, shoe laces
and all his worldly possessions did nothing to improve his
by now depressed but indignant mood. Searching his
pockets he discovered a match. After a few moments
deliberation, he lit the match and carefully introduced it
to the blanket. Immediately, thick black smoke filled the
cell and in his words "all hell let loose". He was dragged
from the cell and the smouldering blanket extinguished.
The next morning as he sat in the ante room awaiting his
court appearance along with drunks, flea ridden down
and outs and prostitutes, he had plenty of time to reflect
on his catalogue of disasters. As he stood, head bowed,
in his crumpled designer suit in front of the magistrate, I
couldn't help feeling sorry for him. He paid his fine and
quickly left to merge into the anonymity of the Glasgow

streets.

I learned very quickly in my service never to take my eyes off a suspect or accused even for a second.   A woman had been arrested for a Breach of the Peace. She was known to be unstable and was being detained in an observation cell.   All items with which she could harm herself had been removed and my duty was merely to sit outside the cell and watch her.   She was in a talkative mood and I listened to her ramblings both happy and sad as she held my hands in hers.   It was a warm afternoon and time was passing very slowly.   After a few hours, a policeman appeared with two ice creams.   I decided to wash my hands in the adjacent room.   On my return only seconds later, the lady was lying on the concrete floor. The turnkey quickly unlocked the door and we rushed over to her.   In those few unguarded moments, she had pulled the elastic from her knickers and tied it around her neck. I cut the elastic and almost immediately she recovered, completely oblivious as to what she had done.   I was very fortunate as the matter never got to the ears of those in charge, but it was a salutary lesson.

In many of the afternoon trials, the accused defended themselves.   They would adopt a posture copied from television programmes, gripping their jacket lapels and pacing the floor with frown and pouting lips, occasionally stroking their unshaven, stubble cheek with dirty hand. Usually, however, their conduct and language very quickly let them down and the Stipendiary Magistrate was forced to intervene when questioning was reduced to

"you're lying ya bastard"
"Naw ahm no"

"Aye ye ur"

"Naw ahm no" ....

One accused when asked "who made this allegation?" replied "I am the alligator m'Lord" and on another occasion the Procurator Fiscal was referred to as the Perculatin Fiscal.

Willie, a regular, was adamant that he had not committed a Breach of the Peace. He had merely shouted "oh fuck, here comes the calvary", and wee Jimmy gave the performance of his life on one occasion "yer Lordship, yer gonnae feel soary fur me when ah tell ye whit happened. The wumman doon the sters felt soary fur me". The Stipendiary Magistrate looked over the top of his gold rimmed spectacles "well I think we'll let me be the judge of that James. Shall we proceed. When you're ready".

I was quite disgusted when one accused appeared for trial charged with ill treating his dog by repeatedly kicking it, but I had to smile when, in his defence, he explained "ahm sure yer Worship you wid iv done the same thing. There ah wiz chattin up this burd when the dug crapped at ma feet". The Magistrate with a wry smile commented "while I sympathise with you and hope that your dog's unfortunate behaviour has had no lasting effect on your romantic efforts, I cannot condone your ill treatment of the dog". He was fined and allowed time to pay.

During a particularly long trial, the Stipendiary Magistrate dozed off. As he usually sat contemplating evidence with head bowed and resting on one elbow, it was not immediately obvious, but the slow rhythmic sound of the inhalation and exhalation of air eventually alerted the court officer who banged the court ledger loudly on the desk. The Magistrate's head shot up "guilty". On realising that the trial had not yet concluded and all eyes were staring at him, he growled impatiently "well carry on, carry on".   The verdict some time later was still guilty.

When some accused appeared, it was a family outing for friends and relatives who would sit in the public benches, and like politicians in the House of Commons, murmur approval or disapproval at the unfolding evidence, only to be silenced by the court usher.   In situations like this, the police room behind the court was a hive of activity, checking names against outstanding warrants.   At the conclusion of the trial as they all filed out, a few would be arrested. This usually caused the remainder of the entourage to loudly object and attempt to rescue their loved ones, resulting in them all being locked up.

Around Christmas time, an old Irish worthy was standing before the Stipendiary Magistrate charged yet again with being drunk and incapable. He was admonished and respectfully touched an imaginary cap.   As he shuffled away, Mr Robertson asked "where are you staying just now?"

"Eh, nowhere at the moment Sir".

There was a pause "would you like thirty days?"

The old man visibly straightened and his tired, bloodshot eyes lit up "oh thank you Sir, thank you, you're a gentleman.   That'll be me in for Christmas and New Year".

With raised hand, the Magistrate silenced him "all right, all right.   Take him away officer".

Still chattering about his good fortune he was led away, as Mr Robertson allowed himself a smile and shake of the head before resuming his usual serious expression "next".

Duty at the High Court was obviously very different. Very sombre and serious but fascinating.   The atmosphere was electric as the most eminent and well know names of the legal profession battled it out like gladiators in an arena with those for and those against sitting in the public galleries gazing down on the posturing figures.   With thrust upon thrust a nervous witness could be backed into a corner until finally there was a hush and with the point proved, the discredited witness would leave the court, head bowed.   Sometimes the accused seemed almost superfluous and it felt more as though a battle was being fought to determine the superiority of one legal mind over another.   I remember the late Nicky Fairbairn meeting a colleague who commented "I see one of your witnesses fainted Nicky".   Instantly Nicky replied in his unique inimitable voice "Yes, it must have been my charm and good looks that did it !!"

CHAPTER TEN

SHOPLIFTING DUTY

A 2.00 pm to 9.00 pm shoplifting shift was always busy especially on a Saturday.   Shoplifters could be divided into four categories – youngsters stealing make up and trendy clothes, young mothers stealing baby items, elderly people stealing food and the professional.

Again the changing pattern in society became obvious. Early in my service, children attending Catholic schools were horrified when threatened that their priest would be told of their misdemeanour. It was a successful deterrent. Latterly, however, the threat would result in a shrug of the shoulders.

Parents' attitudes were also very different.   Some, embarrassed and ashamed, would walk ahead ignoring a very tearful child bringing up the rear sniffing that they would never do it again.   Other furious parents would follow their offspring up the road administering their own justice – give (slap) me (slap) a (slap) showing (slap) up (slap).   Occasionally parents would refuse to come to the office for their child or give them a few slaps for getting caught.

Whenever we called at one particular store, we always had to wait until the children were brought to us.   It was only when one parent mentioned that their child had been made to wash dishes while waiting for us that a few enquiries were made.   It transpired that a few years earlier, big John, the points man, had been approached by the staff of this shop, who had two young children in custody for the theft of a small inexpensive item of makeup. They did not want to charge them but merely wanted John to quite literally "put the fear of death into them". As John could not leave his point, he suggested that they be made to wash some dishes and barred from the store. This became the practice and worked well until eventually the management decided that all shoplifters should be prosecuted. The police were then called, in all cases, irrespective of age or amount involved, but the punishment of washing dishes continued.

Although not condoning it, for some mothers it was very difficult. A woman was charged with the theft of four pairs of girls socks, four pairs of boys stockings, and a batman's cape and mask – total value £2.5.2d (approx. £2.27). Her husband was unemployed, suffering from T.B. She earned £6.9/- per week (£6.45), her rent was £1.11.6d a week (£1.57) and she had hire purchase of £1 per week. This left approximately £4 a week to feed and clothe herself, her husband and four children. She only had one previous conviction in 1946 for stealing coal when she had been fined 10/- or 7 days imprisonment.

Although we normally had a very good relationship with the store detectives, the majority of whom were married ex policewomen, this did not apply in the case of one food store. Their head office insisted that all shoplifters be prosecuted and actively encouraged a league table of arrests. It was so sad being called to arrest an elderly person who had never been in any kind of trouble in their lives, breaking their hearts over a moment of temptation, or I quite believe, in some cases, forgetfulness. When they insisted that one old lady be charged with the theft of a packet of gravy cubes, we spoke to our Inspector who suggested to the management that in such cases, surely it would suffice to ban them from the store. I am glad to say they agreed.

If it was suspected that a shoplifter was a professional thief, or previous convictions proved that they were, it was disappointing to have to pass the case to the C.I.D., but very often they allowed us to accompany them on a search of the accused's house which was extremely interesting for us new girls, especially if further stolen goods were recovered, prompting a well done from the C.I.D. officer.

It was on my first Saturday shoplifting duty that I thought my new career was to come to an abrupt end. I discovered that it was the duty of the new girl to make the communal Saturday night meal. To me boiling an egg successfully was a major achievement, but to be told that eight girls, a Sergeant and an Inspector expected soup, steaks, chips and peas, followed by fruit salad, caused me an uncontrollable panic. I was dispatched with my shopping list and the names and location of the dairy, butcher and chippie. Fortunately, the butcher was well used to us calling, but I could not decide how many tins of soup, peas and fruit salad I would require. Again the shop assistant came to my rescue. It was also very disconcerting to have "B" shift Inspector presiding over us that night. Her nickname was "Chiffy" from the word "chiffonier", defined in the dictionary as a tall thing with drawers. I did not know her and as I stood gazing at the assortment of food and the two ring Belling cooker with its small oven, I sensed her like a vulture staring from her perch. The voice came from somewhere near her toes and bellowed the full length of the long room "Is there a problem Maureen?   "No miss" I squeaked as I began in total confusion to set the table and open the tins.   "Don't you think you'd better put the chips in the oven?"   As her head returned to the pile of reports on her desk, Morag quietly sidled up and whispered "chips in the bottom of the oven, fry the steaks two at a time and put them on the tin plate top part of the oven.   When they're all done, put the soup on the ring that's working.   When you've served the soup, put the peas on – got it?"   "I think so" I whispered back, praying silently "oh God, please make it alright".   He must have heard me.   No one complained.

I did feel quite peeved, however, that whenever Dorothy went for the steaks they were always enormous and cost very little.   It was some months later, we found out that she and the butcher had started going out together.   They eventually got married and we were all disappointed as that was the end of the delicious cheap steaks.

CHAPTER ELEVEN

THE GREENOCK RUN

A 2.00 pm to 9.00 pm shift could also be "the Greenock run". This was a favourite duty. Two police-women were detailed to sit in the back of the police van while it called at the various courts to uplift females who had been sentenced to a spell at Gateside Women's prison in Greenock. Usually, the women, most of whom were regulars, were quite resigned to their fate and it was a real study of human nature listening to their conversations. As a non smoker, when I knew I was rostered for this duty the following week, I would watch while on patrol for under age smokers and confiscate their cigarettes and matches, telling them that their parents could call at the police office and retrieve them. Of course they never told their parents and the Greenock clientele thought me extremely generous handing out my cigarettes to them. They in turn would give us snippets of information and the prostitutes would tell us of the appearance of a new young girl or weirdo punter. Most of them felt it was too late for them but wanted to dissuade young girls.

Their stories were varied. One girl told of going to London with a boyfriend. When he ditched her she was penniless. As she wandered the streets, a man offered her cash for the panties she was wearing. In her words "when you hivnae a penny in yer poakit, an a bloke's offerin ye a fortune fur yer durty knickers, thur's nae contest. Ah jist whipped them aff".

Another spoke of marrying at 16 years, an older man

she thought was a real gentleman, but after the wedding when he still had not touched her, she confronted him and he confessed to being homosexual and had only married her to keep up appearances for his family and friends. Again in her words "it did ma nut in. Ah left him, but ah hud naewher tae go, so ah jist thought whit the hell".

In those days the going rate was £3 a short time, £5 a strip, but one old drunken worthy brought in, had a pocketful of sixpences (2½ p), which prompted the comment from one policeman "och Maggie, you're surely worth more than that". She serviced the old men who stayed in the Holm Street model lodging house and had no doubt begun her career charging the aforementioned rates, but it's a hard game and the years had definitely taken their toll. From the good old days, as she described them, of Blythswood Square, she had sunk to the mediocrity of St. Vincent Street, the debasement of Argyle Street and finally into the depths of the abyss – Holm Street and Clyde Street. She was truly a "doon hiller".

I have often wondered why men treat these women with such disdain and address them in such derogatory terms, while that same species who use them are referred to by the respectable name of "client". He commits no offence but she does.

Once we had delivered our prisoners safely, it was the practice in the summer time to buy cakes and lemonade and return to Glasgow via the picturesque country roads, stopping en route to sit out and enjoy a picnic. In the winter, fish suppers replaced the cakes and we would squeeze in beside the male driver and his partner in the front of the van, a cop and policewoman in the passenger seat and a policewoman sitting on the raised, padded engine between the driver and passenger seat. As there was no heating in the back of the van, we would remain in the front, but on reaching the Glasgow boundary would return to the back in case we were spotted by a boss. This picnic routine had gone on for years and our Sergeants were well aware of it, but she must have thought we were abusing the privilege. On this particular day we did not stop, due to the driver having some urgent business to attend to. As we walked into the office, much earlier than usual, Sgt. Ross without raising her head from her paperwork complained "now girls, it didn't take you all that time to get to Greenock and back. Be quicker tomorrow". For a second we thought of protesting, then thought better of it "yes Sgt.".

Listening to the tales of the women prisoners made me realise that you cannot judge them by our moral values. They have their own ethics which are entirely different from ours.

I was at Beechwood Remand Home when one young girl burst into the head lady's office in a very distressed state. Eventually after a lot of calming and coaxing, but with tears still rolling down her cheeks she confided "it's that Anne Marie. She called me a ....". She began howling again "ah cannae say it miss". After more calming and coaxing, the head lady suggested she spell it. Still sniffing, she took a deep breath "Miss, she called me a fucking C O W".

Having been called to a house where a right old rammy was in progress, we arrived just as the drunken husband gave vent to his piece de resistance "yer nuthin but a fuckin, fat, lazy, mingin auld cow". We were all stunned into a moment's silence at this tirade, until the wife screamed back "ahm no fat".

A private detective told me he had been involved in a divorce case. Giving evidence, he was explaining how he and a colleague had gone to a bedroom in a hotel. On knocking the door, it had been answered by a man in his underpants. Beyond him they could see Mrs X lying in bed. His Lordship interrupted "what time of day was it?"

"3.00 pm m'Lord".

"Good heavens, before dinner".

I also spoke to a retired Judge who quite happily told me that he had firmly believed an accused's evidence because he had been so articulate.

CHAPTER TWELVE

GENERAL DUTIES

A 4.00 pm to 11.00 pm was a general duty shift.   We had a very good liaison with the R.S.P.C.C. and would call on each other for assistance.   One evening I accompanied one of their Inspectors to a flat in Monteith Row. An anonymous caller had reported that three children were begging for food from the other residents.   The flat had been sub-let into individual rooms with a communal bathroom and cooker in the hall.   We found a boy of 14 years, a girl of 12 years and a young girl of about 7 years who was lying on a filthy couch.   All were dirty, undernourished and frightened, and the small child, obviously ill, was a bright yellow colour, later diagnosed as jaundice.   The room was stinking, there was no food in the cupboards, and empty liquor bottles lay on the tacky floor.   The R.S.P.C.C. Inspector informed the parents that he was taking the two older children into care and the younger one to hospital.   Neither parent, mumbling through a drunken stupor, objected and the father's only comment was "well, we won't be here when she comes out".   Some time later, I was again involved with the family when the 12 year old girl ran away from the children's home.   We found her a short time later while out on patrol.   It was very sad to find out that she was on her way back to the children's home having visited Monteith Row, only to have her parents in their usual drunken state shouting abuse at her.

Another case involved a 2 year old child found abandoned in a pram at 10.30 pm.   The mother had gone out drinking, leaving the little boy with her boyfriend.   He became fed up and left him with an 11 year old, who took him out, but abandoned him when he met his pals.

When a mother brought her 4 year old daughter into the office, I was horrified when the little girl quite matter of fact told me she had been shagged by the 9 year old boy left to look after her while her mother went out drinking. I was relieved when the doctor's examination showed no signs of obvious interference, but the family circumstances received further attention.

While that little girl knew words beyond her years, this was not the case with a minister's wife.   She answered her 'phone to be informed by a young man that he was having a hard on.   She apologised and asked him to repeat what he had said which he did.   Again she apologised for not understanding him.   This very genteel lady listened as he described it in graphic detail and then very gently told him that she didn't think either she or her husband could help and suggested that he contact his doctor, whereupon HE slammed down the 'phone.   As we suppressed our giggles, in all innocence she told us "I had never heard of this condition, but he sounded as though he was in great pain poor man.   It was my neighbour who told me I should report the matter to you".

By now I was dealing with matters with some degree of confidence, but every now and then I was brought back down to earth.   In December 1964 the policewomen's department had moved to another building at 48 St Andrew's Square, across from our old accommodation.   I had been sent to collect telex messages.   As I approached the lift, I saw a tall man with braid on his hat

– a boss.   Anxious not to offend, I straightened, smiled and gave him my best salute – "Sir".   Hastily and clumsily he transferred the package he was carrying (his evening meal) to his other hand and returned my salute.   We then stood in an awkward silence gazing heavenwards awaiting the arrival of the lift.   After a few moments, he mumbled something and began to walk up the stairs.   The lift came and I collected the telexes from the third floor Information Room.   As I approached the door to leave, it opened and a rather out of breath "boss" appeared.   I drew myself up in preparation for another salute.   "Oh no, not again" he panted brushing past me.   My Sergeant later spoke to me. The Inspector had asked her to tell the fledgling that you don't salute an Inspector, or anyone else indoors.

CHAPTER THIRTEEN

NIGHTSHIFT

On an 11.00 pm to 6.00 am nightshift some girls had great difficulty sleeping during the day.   Fortunately it never affected me, but the well known cure was a dose of night nurse. On my first night shift, an incident took place which now would not be tolerated, but then we accepted without question as part of a new recruit's initiation.   I was sent over to the C.I.D. on some pretext, and was immediately grabbed by the detective officers. The date stamp was imprinted on the top of my leg at the gap above my stockings, and I was then dumped in a large basket placed on top of a desk.   There was nothing indecent about it, although I must admit when my mum spotted it a few days later, I told her it was a bruise.

On a Friday night while walking through the Fish-market to commence duty, I stood on a piece of wood from an old fish box.   Unfortunately it had a protruding nail which penetrated my shoe.   In the policewoman's room I took off my shoe to find it full of blood.   A uniform car was quickly summoned and I was taken to the Royal Infirmary where, much to my embarrassment, the uniformed driver insisted on carrying me, bloody foot held high, into the Casualty Department.   I tried to protest when I found myself facing an inquisitive Friday night audience, but he ignored me muttering "just try and look like you've been assaulted.   They'll be really impressed".

Again in the Fishmarket, I saw a group of people looking in a pub window.   They called me over and I could just see in the gloom, a very drunk woman sitting on her own at a table wailing for someone to let her out.   She had apparently been in the toilet when all the lights had gone out.   It had taken her some time to find her way back to the lounge where she discovered she was the sole occupant and the doors were locked.   I 'phoned from the nearby police box and the key holder was asked to return to the pub, which was going to take some time as he had not yet arrived at his home in Lennoxtown.   I tried to console her but was drowned out by a gathering crowd of merry cronies "haw Annie, it's usually the lavvie auld women get locked in", "help yersel tae a few haufs hen", and "stoap wailin ya eejit an get stuck in".   Eventually they ran out of wise cracks, their interest waned, and with a few words of encouragement, they wandered off, and I could assure her that help was on the way.   A while later, the beat man arrived to take over and I thanked him profusely as it was a cold night.   It was only when I became an older and wiser policewoman, that I realised his attendance coincided with the impending arrival of the key holder who would no doubt offer a free half in appreciation of the Constable's long, cold wait.

My neighbour and I on patrol found an old drunk man lying on the pavement, blood trickling from a gash on his forehead.   The police van took us to the Royal Infirmary, where he sat patiently between us in the casualty area. Then he began to get restless trying to stand up.   "Sit down" I ordered him.   His bloodshot eyes attempted to focus on me "want away".

"Well you can't.   You have to see the doctor".
He settled for a few minutes and then looked at me ear-

nestly again "want away".

"Don't be a nuisance.   Sit there quietly".

A nurse appeared and as she ushered us into a cubicle, he seized her arm, took a deep breath, paused for a second concentrating "want a pee".

On her speedy return with one of those familiar shaped bottles, a huge toothless grin spread across his face "thank you, thank you nurse".

On nightshift there were no policewomen on duty in the divisions. Everything involving females was referred to the policewomen's department at the Central division where there were two girls and a Sergeant on duty.

It was on a nightshift that the majority of serious indecencies and rapes occurred.   We would attend and take initial statements from the female complainer and witnesses, also all relevant items of clothing, and arrange and be present at the police doctor's examination. While we were doing this, the male C.I.D. officers were carrying out investigations into the identification and arrest of the perpetrator.   Rape is a very serious allegation and it was necessary to impress that fact upon the female. We spent considerable time with one girl who insisted she had been raped by an unknown male.   Had she struggled?   Definitely, but, she could give no explanation as to how the few hundred hair pins holding her beehive hair style in place had remained completely intact.   Medical examination found no marks or bruises consistent with a struggle, but it wasn't until next morning when she had time to consider the seriousness of her allegation that she confessed to the divisional policewoman that she had concocted the whole story as she had been afraid of the possible consequences of her previous evening's activities.

On the other hand it was extremely harrowing to see a young girl breaking her heart, her innocence and trust gone forever.   I used to feel very sorry for the father. While a mum could gather her daughter up in her arms, her father would stand not knowing if he would face rejection or cause her further upset if he gave her the cuddle he wanted to.

On being called to a house in the east end of the city, we were faced with a very distressed old lady in her late seventies. She had been visiting a friend and on her return home, had been pushed into the house by someone who had followed her up the stairs and waited quietly until she unlocked the door. He had then raped her. It was difficult to understand how anyone could inflict such a despicable act on this frail little spinster lying on the casualty surgeon's couch, with all her years of modesty now in tatters, whimpering that the examination was just as painful as the assault on her. Later she revealed in her statement that this loathsome creature had apologised on completion of his defilement.

At the end of a long busy night, it was nice to unwind with a cup of tea.   If the milk ran out, it was usual for us to call at the Tontine Hotel, a men's hostel, that was until one morning when the grimy but kindly warden invited us through to the kitchen, "can't see you ladies stuck for a wee drop milk" he told us cheerfully, and proceeded very expertly to prise the top from a new pint, pour some into our jug, make up the difference with some water, replace the top and give it a shake "there now, the C.I.D. boys will never notice the difference.   They collect it when they start early shift" .... We never told them.

CHAPTER FOURTEEN

TULLIALLAN – 2ND STAGE

Almost a year had gone by and I was ready to return to Tulliallan Police College for second stage training.

The private bus left from St. Enoch Square every Sunday night and arrived back on a Friday evening. It was a noisy, entertaining journey and although we had fun as a crowd, a few romances were kindled, myself included. He was a nice fellow whose name I can't remember, but who eventually emigrated to Australia. Another, the proud possessor of a car, began driving me to and from Tulliallan. He got on very well with my parents but .... That romance did not last long either.

There was plenty of time to settle down into college life over the three month period, and although I still found the academic side required a lot of study, there was a different atmosphere. The Sergeants had been reduced in stature, no longer being the Gods of our initial training.

I became particularly friendly with two policewomen, one from Falkirk, and one from Edinburgh. We had a common interest. We fell madly in love with our P.T. instructor. I had returned to Tulliallan as a non swimmer. I could swim and snorkel underwater, but as another P.T. Sergeant told me in his east coast accent "the trick Miss Ingram is to learn to swim on the surface". Gradually I began to swim a few lengths, but the lifesaving proved difficult. I was paired off with another policewoman. I was to teach her to surface dive 14' to retrieve a rubber

brick and she was to teach me the art of rescuing someone. Her surface dives progressed, but she couldn't continue with me constantly drowning her and so poor Malky
became my next victim. He was very patient and had an
amazing lung capacity which enabled him to keep going
as I trawled him underwater. Our swimming lessons took
place at the lovely swimming pool in the naval dockyard
at Rosyth and additional lessons were at the not so lovely
Alloa baths. On our first visit to Rosyth, the policewoman
Sergeant warned us to be vigilant as one of the sailors
was suspected of hiding in a cupboard within the ladies'
changing room. On reflection our actions were probably
a little extreme. The cupboard in question had a row
of drilled holes along the top of the door. As the girls
walked in, one would move along the side of the wall and
on reaching the door quickly push a pen through the holes.
I think it's perhaps fortunate that we never caught him.

Unfortunately, the baths at Alloa had a breakdown of
the filter system. We visited on a Wednesday night just
before or just after sacks of chlorine were added to the
pool. Many times it was impossible to open your eyes in
the morning until bathed in warm water. I also returned
home with four skin infections, but of course it is impossible to ascertain the source. Cops are not known for
their discretion and I remember them referring to one of
my infections as "Maureen's galloping gunga rot !!!!!"

The fact that I gained my intermediate swimming
certificate was entirely due to Sheila and Malky's val-
iant efforts and my own perseverance and dedication in
trying to impress our hero Sgt. Mills. This was also the
reason for myself, Margaret and June coming in first,
second and third on our final three mile run.

During the course, I discovered that gin was not the drink for me. We were celebrating the end of an exam in the college bar, and being pretty riotous I suspect. Sgt. Mills came in enquiring as to the reasons for our jollification as our results were pathetic. I promptly burst into tears and no amount of comforting or assurance that I had not done badly could stem the flood of tears. I was helped by Sgt. Mills, June and Margaret to the bottom of the stairs leading to the policewomen's accommodation beyond which no male was permitted to venture. On handing me over into the safe custody of the waiting policewoman Sergeant and much to the envy of Margaret and June, Sgt. Mills pecked me on the cheek, patted my shoulder and squeezed my hand, obviously regretting having ever poked his nose inside the bar. The next morning I remembered little of the momentous moment, but suffered greatly the embarrassment and never touched another gin.

It was a common occurrence for the second stage to play jokes on the first stage girls. One night we went round all the rooms telling them that the fire alarm had activated and we were to muster at the front of the castle, an area off limits to students. Of course we were fully clothed, but we marched the girls outside in nighties, dressing gowns, hair rollers and creamy faces. A few minutes after we abandoned them standing to attention, they realised their mistake and had to pass a gathering of very bemused senior ranking overseas students on their return to our quarters. Their revenge was sweet, however, when a few nights later, they cornered me and dumped me fully clothed into a cold water bath.

All too soon, three months had passed, the exams had

been sat and we were standing on the parade ground in our bulled shoes and pressed uniforms being inspected for the last time by the Commandant of the police college. The march, passed the dignitaries on the raised dais, ended the next stage of our probation and after exchanging addresses with June and Margaret, with whom I later went on holiday, I returned home to resume duty at the policewomen's department.

CHAPTER FIFTEEN

THE POLICEWOMEN'S DEPT.

Although college was over, I arrived back to find that the policewomen were to be inspected by Her Majesty's Inspector of Forces – a really big occasion.   Once again, uniforms etc. were given the Tulliallan treatment and days were spent making sure that everything in the office was perfect.   On the big day in the muster hall, I found myself standing at attention in the front row, opposite the full length mirror, allowing me the opportunity of studying our V.I.P. as he proceeded along the back row.   As he turned to view the rear of number two row, our eyes met.   Quickly I averted my gaze to the floor, but as curiosity got the better of me, I allowed myself another glance in the mirror, only to find him still watching me.   Again I diverted my gaze.   When he finally reached me he leant forward "do I meet with your approval miss?"   Blushing uncontrollably, I nodded "yes Sir."   "Thank you".

He smiled and continued, followed by the entourage of policewoman Superintendent, Chief Inspector and two Inspectors all looking at me very suspiciously as they passed.   On being quizzed later by the Superintendent I lied "I couldn't really make out what he said Mrs Beattie".

This incident pales into insignificance when compared with Mairi on a C.I.D. course parade at Tulliallan.   Being the only female there, the Commandant stopped to speak to her.   His eyes immediately fell on a brooch of a pink cat pinned on the lapel of her jacket.   "Tell me", he said loudly in his very affected accent "is there any significance in your pink pussy". Immediately realising what he had said, he marched quickly to the end of the row and dismissed the parade with a wave of his hand.

A Sunday morning was usually a quiet time, allowing the divisional driver to clean and polish the interior and exterior of his police car. I was sent with Donald, the driver, to a shop in Howard Street where a young boy had been found wandering. When we arrived, Leslie, accompanied by a happy, black, hairy mongrel, was enjoying a bar of chocolate. Donald groaned as sticky fingers clutched the seats and Heinz' pink tongue slapped his lips and panted on the windows.   Enquiring as to where they stayed, directed us to the south side of the river, and after some prompting, Leslie gripped Donald's arm "here".   As we followed them up the stairs, a breathless Donald pondered why everything happened on the top floor, to which I had no answer, but had to agree, it seemed to be the case. Sunday mornings are not a good time to try and arouse Gorbals residents, and it was some time before our combined hammering on the door produced any result. A bleary eyed apparition in vest and pants eventually appeared "whit ye wantin?"

"One son and one dug" growled Donald

"No mine pal" and the door slammed shut.

Back at the office, the on duty Inspector smiled "I know you Leslie.   Have you been getting a nice ride in a police car again?"

Leslie beamed and nodded his head vigorously.   Armed with the correct address, we delivered him to his top flat house and on determining that he was indeed one of their brood, wasted no time in beating a retreat.   How-

ever, on reaching the bottom of the stairs, we heard
the door opening and a yowl "where did you pick up
that filthy mutt".   There was another yowl and the door
banged shut.   We looked at each other, hastily climbed
into the car and drove off.

Donald's neighbour was apparently a bit of a man about
town, but unfortunately I rather tarnished his image.
They were giving me a lift for the Sunday morning rolls
and milk.   On the previous night, Maggie and I had
spotted Ian going into the Albert Ballroom.   Innocently
I asked him if he had enjoyed himself at the Albert.   He
froze and his neck turned red.   Donald looked in the rear
view mirror "Where?"

"The Albert Ballroom".

Donald burst out laughing "and you told me and the boys
you'd won a fortune at the casino".

Needless to say I never got a lift again when Ian was
driving the car.

About this time, our shift pattern was altered.   Nightshift ended at 6.00 am on Monday morning and late shift
commenced at 4.00 pm that day.   Late shift then ended
at 11.00 pm and early shift began at 7.00 am on Tuesday
morning.   Travelling home one Tuesday at the end of my
duty, I was sitting on the bench seat in the middle of the
bus.   I nodded off and my head rolled back.   I immediately sat upright and realised I had no hat.   Cautiously
I turned to find it wedged firmly in the narrow window
frame.   Prising it free, I looked around and found only
one man watching who gave me a sympathetic smile and
winked slowly.

Parties were still plentiful as policewomen departed to
get married.   Three policemen who eventually left and

later became the group Gaberlunzie would bring along their instruments and a good sing song fun night was guaranteed.

After one of these social occasions, I had only a couple of hours sleep. I reported for duty at 6.45 am trying my best to appear bright eyed and bushy tailed, but the Sergeant's comment shattered that illusion. "Do you intend to spend the whole of early shift like that Maureen?"

"Sergeant?"

"Look in the mirror"

There to my horror, I saw only a shiny brass collar stud – no collar – no tie.

"Sort it out" she instructed.

I succeeded in procuring a paper collar several sizes too big, but no one had a spare tie. With a little ingenuity, we cut the back off my neighbour's tie, made a little knot and secured it to my neck with a piece of string. I spent the entire shift avoiding anyone of rank.

On days off, a group of us usually went to the Bier Keller in Union Street. One night, a small elderly man sat at the end of our bench table. As the evening wore on, Grace became more and more concerned for this sad, lonely, little character, while I became more and more convinced that I knew him. As we were leaving, Grace who had begun talking to him, took his hands in hers, telling him to take care. He then gave her a kiss. The next day on duty, I began looking through my collection of criminal's photographs and there he was. I confirmed it with the other girls and we then let Grace see it "That nice wee man. What's he done?" Slowly I turned over the photograph to reveal that Alfie was one of Glasgow's prolific abortionists. (Abortion was illegal, until the Abortion

Act of 1967 made it legal under certain circumstances. Prior to 1967, there were many back street abortionists).   Grace shot off and we discovered her in the toilet scrubbing her hands and mouth spluttering "and I kissed him".

After I returned from college, I developed a troublesome back pain and was advised to place a plank of wood under my mattress.   The police at that time was a sort of self help group.   We had ex joiners, builders, plasterers, plumbers and painters, and if they couldn't help, they knew someone who could.   In my case, the divisional van driver had a friend who could supply the wood.   When I finished early shift, we went to a yard and loaded the van.   Unfortunately, on our way to my house, the driver received a radio message to pick up a male prisoner.   We managed to squeeze him in beside my plank of wood and he was quite docile, at one point commenting "is it no an awfi lang wey tae the jile the day".   As we neared my house, the driver braked suddenly.   All the years that board was under my mattress, it bore the skid marks of the drunk's dirty hands and feet as he slid along its full length.

Some people have seriously asked me if we get lessons in patience and control at college.   We don't and sometimes it can be extremely difficult.

As an animal lover, I was appalled to be confronted with two young boys who had just thrown a puppy to its death from the top storey of the Mitchell Street car park. On asking them why, without any flicker of remorse, they impatiently pulled a face, tutted and shrugged their shoulders.

One day, a reporter and photographer from The Weekly News arrived at the office.   They were doing a feature on presenting bouquets of flowers to deserving people and the local beat man had nominated the policewomen.   I was volunteered by the Sergeant to accept them on behalf of the department.   It was a very nice gesture, but unfortunate that I am not at all photogenic.

Frequently on a late shift, I would miss my last bus which necessitated catching a later one. This stopped about two miles from my home.   However, I had become friendly with two of our local beat men, and when Roy and Hugh were on nightshift, they would carry out their check on the shops at the bus stop to coincide with my arrival. If it was a quiet night they would call in for a quick cuppa much to the delight of my dad, who was now in poor health.

On 7 June 1965, almost on completion of my probationary period, I learned I was being transferred to the Information Room.

CHAPTER SIXTEEN

INFORMATION ROOM

The Information Room, which later, on moving to police Headquarters at Pitt Street, was re-named the Control Room, was situated on the third floor of the Central divisional offices in Turnbull Street.   The first thing I noticed on entering, was the continual chattering of the telex machine, a noise which was even evident in the small adjoining dining room/kitchen. The main office had a long conveyor belt running down its full length, with switchboards on either side which buzzed incessantly on a Friday and Saturday night.   All telephone messages were placed on the belt where they trundled to one end to be perused by the Inspector and if non urgent, would trundle back along the belt to a room which broadcast to Glasgow based cars for attention.   If the message was relevant to areas outwith Glasgow, it was then given to an adjoining room for transmission to operators in those areas who in turn passed it to their area cars.

On my introduction to Inspector Bogue on my first day, I had to promise not to salute him.

Operating the telex machine did not pose much of a problem for me with my knowledge of typing, but my first broadcast was nerve racking, more so because I knew my dad had our radio tuned in to listen to me, something he continued to do, particularly if we had visitors.   I was circulating a stolen car and began as instructed "To ZH (Edinburgh), GR (Renfrewshire), GL (Lanarkshire), AB (Ayrshire), AK (Dunbartonshire) and AH (Stirlingshire) …. Stolen between …etc. etc.   When I asked for acknowledgement of my message, the female ZH operator snapped that I had not dictated the message at dictation speed. I was shell shocked until first GR, followed by GL and then the rest of the male operators confirmed that they had received the message and added a welcome.   I was later told that this particular lady did not like other female operators to be on the air.

Policewomen, who were seconded to the Information Room were not generally allowed to operate the switchboards or the Glasgow room, but one Sunday morning I was with Donald, who was very highland.   Normally, he was a quiet, calm person, but he became extremely frustrated when, due apparently to freak atmospheric conditions, we were receiving calls from pilots requesting permission to land at Prestwick Airport. Eventually Donald could contain himself no longer "would the American pilot please stand by. This is the City of Glasgow Police Information Room attempting to pass a message to one of its cars".   We never found out if he received our message, but visualised a plane circling Prestwick Airport, waiting patiently for Donald to complete his broadcast.

Much later, on touring the new Control Room at Pitt Street, I could see why it was nicknamed Star Ship Enterprise. Computers, consuls, and flashing lights had replaced the old conveyor belt and buzzing switchboards, and the area was brightly lit and spacious. Gone was the cosy wee totally inadequate dining room with its steamed up window and dirty, noisy, deficient X-pelair, where Ella would stand on a chair and give us an impromptu concert of arias from her amateur operatic club's latest show, while we crushed together at the impractical table eating our soup and sandwiches, or beans on toast.

Modernisation was inevitable and necessary, but our wee Information Room was never called Disneyland, because "this disnae work and that disnae work"!!!!!(Since then, the Control Room has been updated several times).

Meantime, our socialising had begun to centre around the Odeon cinema who were featuring the big stars of the day. Thanks to the beat Constable who allowed us in the stage door, I was able to meet and obtain autographs from Val Doonican, Engelbert Humperdink, Tom Jones, Roy Orbison, The Rolling Stones, Ike and Tina Turner and many more.

After a year, I returned to the policewomen's department, my probationary period complete, and three months later was posted to the Southern Division at Craigie Street.

CHAPTER SEVENTEEN

THE SOUTHERN DIVISION –
CRAIGIE STREET

At the Southern Division there were two C.I.D. girls and three policewomen. As one policewoman went on parking duty to the Central Division every week, in effect two policewomen covered an early and a late shift. We all occupied one large room, C.I.D. girls on one side at a desk beside the window and the policewomen at the other side facing the door. The C.I.D. male officers were in an adjacent room.

My first duty was directing traffic at the junction of Titwood Road and Darnley Road, near the site of Cross-myloof Ice Rink. It was an awkward crossing, but the experienced policeman who drove me there gave me some invaluable advice. Always study and plan the crossing before stepping out on to it, and, if you do get in a mess, look at your watch and purposefully walk off. I frequently used his first piece of advice, and probably for that reason, never had to follow the latter.

In the police, you are constantly surprised at the attitude of people. I was at a crossing in Victoria Road and had stopped the traffic in both directions. On my signal, the schoolchildren began to cross the road, when a fast moving car drove up the inside lane, narrowly missing the children and turned left into a side street. I blew my whistle, but on approaching the vehicle expecting to find a very shocked and apologetic driver, I was confronted by an extremely rude, indignant lady complaining that I was delaying her from collecting her children from school. She was completely oblivious to the fact that a tragedy had almost occurred and threatened to report me, when I commented that being late for her own children, did not give her the right to mow down other children.

The social scene continued and promotions, retirements, births and marriages were all celebrated. The turnkey was an excellent baker and a small contribution produced some wonderful buffets.

As the evening progressed at my first "pay off", some of the C.I.D. boys were deciding who was going to ensure that I got home "safely". Poor Jimmy. I insisted on walking the four miles home, thanked him and said goodnight. He couldn't get a taxi and ended up walking another four miles back to the office. I don't think it was quite what he had planned, but he managed to laugh about it later.

I found missing persons enquiries extremely interesting. It was very satisfying, gleaning information from friends and relatives, and piecing together the jigsaw, resulting in the person being traced.

When a fourteen year old boy went missing, enquiries eventually led me to the north side of the city, where I interviewed a New Zealand gentleman. He was gorgeous, but there was something about his story …..I arranged for him to call at the office the next day and told the C.I.D. girls and the typists about the dishy guy with the hypnotic blue eyes and wonderful tan. They turned out in force to watch him arriving at the office. I spent a while with him, much to the amusement of my colleagues who questioned my motives, but I still wasn't satisfied with his story, and told the Detective Inspector who interviewed him. After about two or three minutes, he emerged from the room "your gorgeous baby blue eyed poof is in tears and wants to tell the nice policewoman all about it".   His information resulted in us tracing the boy who was returned home unharmed to the relief of his parents.

We were not so successful on one enquiry in Castlemilk.   A lady taking in her washing heard a whistle.   She turned and was confronted by a youth wearing only a jumper pulled over his face, performing a "little jig". He disappeared before the astonished woman could do anything.   A few days later, another lady was looking out of her kitchen window when a fellow similarly attired stepped from behind her garage and performed "a dinky little dance" before disappearing.   The complaints mounted up and despite plain clothes patrols, he was never caught.

While in a house in Castlemilk on a missing person enquiry, I was bitten by their pet dog.   It barely grazed my skin, but the land rover crew insisted on taking me to the Victoria Infirmary for an anti tetanus injection.   I could hardly walk afterwards, and vowed I was not returning for the booster jab.   I had soon forgotten about it, when I was instructed by the officer on duty one day, to call at the Victoria Infirmary to take a statement from a road accident victim.   One of the land rover crew came with me and spoke to the lady at the casualty desk.   A nurse then appeared and ushered me into a cubicle.   As I was about to enquire as to the apparent absence of the patient, a doctor appeared "so, you're the young lady who wasn't coming back for her anti tetanus booster!!!!"

A little lady suffering from periodic delusions adopted me.   Apparently she would not leave her home to go into residential care and was not ill enough for the decision to be made for her.   She always insisted on seeing me and would show me the ripped soles of her shoes, her teeth which she had blackened, and rancid bottles of milk.   In her mind, they were all caused by the bad men who got into her house through the wardrobe.   I would calm her down and tell her that I had replaced the milkman and postman with undercover agents.   This would satisfy her and allay her fears for another few weeks.   When I eventually left the Southern Division, my male colleagues told her that I had left the police and was working in a Soho night club. However she became so distressed, they had to confess that I had moved back to the policewomen's department at Headquarters.   She never did call there, but I received a lovely, lucid letter from her, along with some handkerchiefs and a comb in a leather case bearing my name.   I learned later that she had finally gone into a nursing home. I didn't visit in case it upset her, but sent Christmas cards and holiday postcards.   Eventually one Christmas when I telephoned the home, I was told she had died.

Never having been to a football match, I was quite excited when I was told I was to be on duty at Hampden Park for a Rangers/Celtic match.   My enthusiasm soon turned to disappointment, when I was allocated the first aid room, a cold barren place beneath the stand, and could only listen to the cheers as I took details from a man with a cut nose caused when the football hit him and broke his spectacles.

One night, after a quiet late shift, two of the uniform drivers gave me a lift home.   They came in for a cup of tea, and during a chat with my mum and dad, it transpired that the father of one of them had been in the

Springburn Harriers. My dad, who was not at all well, had also belonged to that club and he had a wonderful time reminiscing. When they left, he declared it the best night he had enjoyed for a long while. The next morning, 5 January 1967, my mum called me through to the bedroom. He had died in his sleep. He was 59 years old. I have never forgotten the wonderful understanding and genuine sympathy of all my colleagues at the Southern Division. When I returned to work, one of the C.I.D. girls asked me if I wanted to go out for a drink. Mairi, my counterpart in uniform had just broken off her engagement, and Liz decided it would be a good idea for the three of us to get together. That evening began a friendship which is now in its 35th year.

One morning I was called into the Chief Superintendent's room and told I was going on a three week police driving course. In the class at Helen Street, I studied the first question on the form in front of me "how many years driving experience?" I wrote down my answer and returned it to the instructor who studied it for a few minutes "what do you mean 17 hours?"

"My driving lessons".

"And you haven't driven since?"

"No".

He sighed and raised his eyes to heaven. That afternoon I warily eased myself into the massive Zephyr 6 with its enormous steering wheel, hand brake on the right side by the door and elaborate column change gear stick. My classmates sat silently in the back, relieved that they weren't first. "I've never driven a car like this" I shouted nervously to the instructor sitting about a mile away at the other end of the long bench seat.

"Well, there's a first time for everything. Now, first and second, pull towards you, third and fourth, push away from you. Reverse we'll do later".

And off we went. Well, not quite as smoothly as that.

"I will drive this vehicle according to the system of car control. Seat belts securely fastened, mirror, signal, mirror", and off we went with a crunch, crunch of gears. It didn't go too badly, except when I ever so gently scraped the front bumper along a cemetery wall. The instructor was very understanding and assured me it wasn't even enough to merit any repair. After several days of intense instruction we were driving along a disused road changing gear with a carton of water sitting on the bonnet.

From our trusty Zephyr, we moved on to manoeuvrability lessons in an old police van. I had to be propped up with cushions and even then found the steering so stiff, I had to stand up to haul the steering wheel round. At the test, I reached the last obstacle, but was running out of time and made the decision to demolish the last cone rather than try and reverse. Alex was a little concerned "if that had been a pedestrian, what would you have done?"

"Definitely reversed and incurred a time penalty".

"I'm relieved to hear that" he replied sarcastically.

For the last part of our course, we were taken to Tulliallan Police College for the day and taught basic procedures for correcting a skid at the Advanced Drivers skid pan (all traffic department drivers undertake an intensive driving course at Tulliallan).

The day before our final test, Alex admitted that it had been easier to teach me than some of the experienced drivers, as I had not developed any bad habits which had to be corrected. However, he felt I needed more driving practice and arranged for one of his mates in the Traffic Department to take me out that evening in his own car. I thought it would be for an hour probably. Four hours later, I returned home to a worried mum. I was absolutely exhausted. I had been on dual carriageways, country roads, lanes, obstacle courses, up and down gears, reversing. It worked. The next day I passed. I was a police driver.

Several people suggested that I buy a car as my mum's health was getting worse and it would be easier for us to get around. Eventually, I felt that my finances were sound enough and again the self help group rallied round. Alex was an expert and we visited several garages. I was always grateful, but slightly embarrassed when he kicked tyres, shook his head as he surveyed an engine, drove the poor cars over cobbled streets, only to end up dashing the salesman's hopes. A nice, shiny, maroon A40 took my fancy and Alex once again gave it his close scrutiny. After much stroking of his chin and sighing, he turned to the salesman "we'll take it". My heart leapt, "but only if you put on four new tyres". There was a pause. "O.K., agreed" nodded the salesman. I was the proud owner of my first car which ran for years.

My dad, through necessity, had been a keen and competent D.I.Y. enthusiast and retained everything "in case it came in handy". I decided the time had come to clear out the shed and garage. When I told my mum that I intended to take all the old bits of metal to a scrap dealer, she asked if she could come, never having seen one. I got her dressed in her old gardening coat and she sat excitedly as we drove into the yard to be greeted by "whit uv ye goat hen.   It's no knoaked aff is it?"   I assured him it wasn't, and he began to weigh our little bundles of brass, copper, etc.

The next morning sitting in the office, one of the plain clothes officers came in "so what were you flogging at the scrappies then?"   They had been carrying out observations on the place when my little A40 came toodling along.   When I told my mum, she was mortified "what will they think of me in that old coat!".   Mairi and Liz thought it was hilarious.

In those days, we received a monthly salary and it was collected from divisional headquarters against your signature.   On days off, most of the men would arrive with their children, their wives' way of preventing them going for a drink with their mates.   However, they reckoned without Mairi who had qualified as a children's nurse prior to joining the police and was more than delighted to entertain a few children, while their dads slipped off for a quick pint.

While working in the Southern Division, our policewoman Superintendent Mrs Beattie retired, and was replaced by Miss Kay, who decided to pay us a visit. As she stood inspecting our room expressing her surprise that we had no lockers or even a locked drawer for our personal use, she rested her hand on the top drawer of the filing cabinet to emphasize the point.   The next few minutes dragged on like hours and a nervous cough tickled my dry throat.   When she eventually left, I collapsed in a chair, unable for a moment to explain to the girls.   They were puzzled, until I opened the top drawer of the filing cabinet – my drawer – to reveal a collection of bottles containing varying amounts of alcohol from the last pay off.

The Eastern Division had introduced a team of plain clothes officers patrolling in an old van, which had proved very effective and became known as "The Untouchables". It was decided that a similar venture should be set up in the Southern Division for a five week period under the leadership of Detective Inspector Watson.   I was absolutely thrilled when the D.I. asked for me to be part of the squad.   When my mum saw me dressed for the part, she asked if that was why we were called "The Untouchables". The D.I. with many years service knew every crook in the south side.   He sat in the back of our battered old van shouting out orders.   "Him, follow him.   He'll be up to something", and out I would jump.   He was a hard taskmaster, but we all learned a lot from him.   One day, I followed a well known housebreaker for quite a distance, until he turned into the entrance to a group of flats.   The van duly arrived, but my tail was soon very much between my legs.

"Which flat did he go into, or did he cut through the backs into the square?"
Of course I didn't know.   We toured around but never found him.

"You realise you've lost him.   He's probably doing some poor wee soul's house right now" he growled, as I sat fighting back a tear.

A few days later, I was following a ned when he stopped beside a van being unloaded.   In a second he had one of the parcels and was off through a close.   I was after him like a whippet.   I heard the D.I.'s voice resonating around the close walls "Smithie, you might as well stop.   I was jailing your paw before you were born".   The ned paused and I had him. He was a big hefty guy, but was stunned at being gripped by a 5'5" snarling terrier determined not to let him go. As he was bundled into the van, a faint smile crossed the D.I.'s face "well done wee one. You're learning" ....I was elated.

Roy and I being about the same age, were usually partnered as a couple and would stroll along the street hand in hand. On one such occasion, Roy spotted his next door neighbour walking towards us. Noticing us, he began to study a shop window intently, but as we passed, Roy greeted him. The poor fellow was so embarrassed, he mumbled a reply while gazing at the ground and rushed on. We had a good laugh, but on returning to the office, Roy decided he had better 'phone his wife to explain that we were working. Roy was a really nice guy liked by all the policewomen. He would come to the policewomen's room anytime for a cup of tea and a biscuit, but this used to puzzle one of the other cops who used to comment in a good humoured way "how come you give him a cup of tea. I never get one and I'm much better looking!".

Too soon, it was the last day of our squad. We had 99 arrests to our credit and spent the whole morning searching for another case to make it the magical 100. Finally we spotted a young lad with a bag about to enter a scrap yard. We pounced but as we gazed at the pathetic little scraps of lead stolen from his work, and then at each other, we made a decision. Our total remained at 99.

As we were disbanding and returning to our various duties, we decided on a farewell drink. I made the fatal mistake of trying to impress the D.I. that I could keep up with the boys. Later, on being put to bed by Eric's wife,

I can vaguely remember her giving them a row for getting me in that state – well us females have to stick together !!!. After a couple of hours sleep, I was driven home by the teetotaller in the group and deposited on my door step. My mum took one look at me.

"I don't suppose you'll be wanting your tea?"

"What is it?"

"Liver and onions!"

I didn't reply. I took a slightly curved route to my bedroom via the bathroom and was ever so grateful that the bed stopped spinning long enough for me to collapse on to it. In the decidedly frosty atmosphere the next morning, my mother's only comment was "In all the years I was married to your father, he never came home in a state like that".

A few months later, Mairi and I were a bit apprehensive when the Chief Superintendent called us to his room, but nothing had prepared us for the devastating news. The new policewoman Superintendent had begun a policy of job rotation, and we were being recalled to the policewomen's department. We were both in tears, which prompted Mr. Murchie to telephone Miss Kay and ask her to reconsider, but the lady was not for turning, and so it was with very heavy hearts that Mairi and I bade farewell to the Southern Division.

CHAPTER EIGHTEEN

P.W. DEPT. – REVISITED

On 9th October 1967, my first day back in the police-woman's department, I was informed that my main duty was to be driver to our Superintendent.

I also quickly learned that while our previous Superintendent had been referred to as Mrs Beattie, our new Superintendent insisted that we call her ma'am.

Our vehicle, which had been supplied to the police-woman's department in December 1964 was a bottle green Hillman Minx and our call sign was Mike 10. As the dog section van was Mike 8, we were commonly referred to as the dog van and the bitch van.

Shortly after I began my new post, ma'am ordered me to study a certain chapter of the Instruction Book. The next day on driving her to a ladies meeting where she was giving a talk, I duly carried out the appropriate order in the Instruction Manual, holding open the car door and saluting her as she entered and exited the vehicle. I then, as commanded, remained in the vehicle for two hours, despite all efforts by the hall keeper to entice me into his office for a cup of tea. Even the divisional male Superintendent's drivers commented that she was the only Superintendent who insisted on this practice.

I hated being her driver and developed a few annoying habits which she was never quite able to prove were deliberate. She was rather plump and in those days seat belts were adjusted manually. I would make sure that the seat belt was positioned for a slim person and wait patiently as she fumbled to re-adjust it.   She did once comment "I always seem to get into this car after one of the skinnier girls has been in it", but I said nothing. I also became quite an expert at parking, making it a difficult long step from the car to the pavement, but an equally difficult short step into the gutter first.

Our Chief Inspector nearing the end of her career, was a nice inoffensive little lady who nursed her ailing mother.   Ma'am would instruct me to take her some-where and order Miss Law to remain in the office until she returned, which was always well after the Chief Inspector's finishing time.   On her return, she would dismiss her and Miss Law would rush off to catch a bus. On quite a few occasions, my neighbour and I would ask the Sergeant if we could go out on a mobile patrol.   She would ascertain that ma'am was finished with the car for the day and we would then race round to the bus stop and give Miss Law a lift home.   The only redeeming factor about being ma'am's driver was that after she fin-ished duty, we were able to utilise the vehicle.

We had cause one night to be grateful to a member of the public.   In Stoneyhurst Street, we were waved down by a man complaining that youths had smashed the window of a nearby hall.   He pointed out one of the neds who immediately took to his heels.   I pursued him on foot through closes, back courts, across streets, up hills. Occasionally he would stop, but as I reached him, off he would go again.   Eventually he gave up, and I ordered him in short staccato breaths to drop the bottle he was carrying.   Fortunately, he was as exhausted as me, and did so.   I marched him down to Saracen Street where I was joined by my neighbour who had only recently returned to work after a serious illness. We were immediately surrounded by his friends including his girlfriend who was encouraging the group to rescue him and with much bravado knocked Myra's hat to the ground. We managed to get our backs to some railings and then heard the welcome sound of a police siren. The crowd scattered but Myra grabbed the girlfriend. We discovered at the office that the ned was an abscondee and it was a bus driver who had made a 999 call from the police box at Saracen Cross.

About 3.00 am I was being driven by the policewoman Sergeant about 10 miles an hour up one of the Glasgow streets looking for any young girls hanging around the prostitute area. A taxi driver approaching us flashed his lights, and thinking he was about to report something, we stopped alongside.

"You're going the wrong way. It's a one way street".
As quick as a flash the sergeant replied "Thanks, but it's O.K. we're chasing someone".

During another nightshift, my neighbour and I spotted a man climbing out of a pub window in London Road. We leapt out and I grabbed him and threw him into the back of the car. Myra began chasing after a second man who had jumped from the window. Some colleagues arrived and I pointed them in the direction that Myra had taken. It was only then that I turned my attention to the ned in the back seat.

"Been in bother before?"

"Aye, jist a couple of serious assaults"

"Well just sit there and don't give me any hassle".
To his credit he didn't. He was more anxious about what his pals would say when they discovered he'd been

arrested by a lassie! (Remember this was long before integration). A few minutes later, the other car returned with Myra and the second housebreaker. They had been quite concerned when they learned from Myra that in their concern for her, they had unintentionally left me with the first prisoner. Myra and I later received the Chief Constable's commendation for that little episode.

Around this time, I was involved in a few plain clothes jobs. County cars were not allowed to pick up passengers at random within the city boundaries. Two policewomen would wander around the main streets and the Hackney Branch, who governed the Glasgow city cabs, would pounce if we were successful in flagging down a county cab. I always felt sorry for these drivers, knowing that if I had been genuinely looking for a taxi after a night out, I would have been delighted to see one approaching, irrespective of whether he was a hackney or private hire.

Unlicensed dance halls were another target for plain clothes officers. Margaret (previously mentioned in the cat kitty story) and I were a popular choice with my build and Margaret's long black hair.

I went into a pub in St Enoch Square along with Jimmy, my date for the evening, prior to us attempting to get into an unlicensed disco near George Square. As I sat down, I noticed the barman watching us. Peem, as he was known as, went over to order a drink, but after a few minutes of very serious conversation he returned minus the drink. "C'mon, he's asked us to leave". Outside he explained that the barman had told him he didn't want our type in his bar. As it was necessary for us to smell of drink, we then went to another rather salubrious pub in Midland Street, where we mingled perfectly.

We gained access to the disco without any problem and began our other task which was to identify a rather vicious ned wanted on warrant who had "TONGS" tattooed on his fingers.   We also had to be alert to the possibility of a past "customer" recognising us as police officers.   We were standing at the bar when simultaneously we spotted on the opposite side, a ned fitting the description.   Raising his glass to his lips, there for all to see were the tell tale initials on his fingers.   As the uniform officers burst in, I made my way to the cloakroom as arranged, to collect our jackets, as Peem indicated the whereabouts of the suspect, and made his way to the door, the idea being for us both to slip out unnoticed. However, as the saying goes "the best laid plans ......" The cloakroom attendant told me that the polis weren't letting anyone leave, and insisted that I stand beside her. It was a very confused policeman who took down my fictitious name and address, while the attendant assured him "ahm jist the cloakroom wumman by the way and she's the wee lassie that helps me oot".   I was relieved when the owner pled guilty and it was unnecessary for us to attend court.

In an unlicensed night club, John and I ordered wine with our meal, but were told they weren't licensed to sell drink.   We were beginning to wonder if the information had been correct as we could see no-one with glasses on the table.   When we finished our meal, John tried again to order drinks, and this time we were told they only had gin or whisky.   John ordered and a few minutes later our drinks arrived in coffee cups.   We then became aware of the amount of "coffee" our fellow diners appeared to

be consuming.   We settled down to watch the cabaret.
With feeling, a young lady began the English translation
of "Hava N'gilah".....''Now is the moment, now .....".   She
got no further as the door burst open and uniform police
officers took up positions around the restaurant.   Chief
Inspector Lees took the microphone from the astonished
singer and instructed everyone to remain seated.   At
the conclusion of the operation when the police left,
John and I felt quite guilty as the manager apologised to
everyone for their spoiled evening and announced that
no-one would be charged for their meal.

I also began working in some minor drugs operations.
On searching a flat during a party, I found a substance
which later proved to be cannabis.   I was quite delighted
and amused when not only was I congratulated by the
drugs officers but also by the owner of the flat.   "Aye
well done, ah never thought anyone would have found
that".   His guests who were totally unperturbed and all
in high spirits with the wacky backy also added their
congratulations.

A not so successful job was when Myra and I were
sent into a chemist's shop in the Partick area of the
city.   Information had been received that the owner was
selling Preludin to schoolchildren.   Glancing around, I
asked him confidentially in my broadest Glasgow accent
"Goat any prellies?"

"I beg your pardon" he replied politely.

"Prellies, know whit ah mean?"

"Pardon?"

"PRELLIES"

"I'm sorry I don't know what you're talking about".

I suspected we were on to a loser but continued
valiantly

"Want me tae spell it out – PRELUDIN – we know you've got some.   Wur pals goat some from ye".

The poor man went apoplectic as he stuttered to find his voice. We were then subjected to a lengthy lecture about ruining our young lives as we backed out of the door making our escape.

One very sad occasion has remained vividly in my mind.

About 4.00 pm on Monday 3rd November 1969, the security staff at the S.T.V. Studios in Hope Street (now the Theatre Royal Opera House) were alerted by an automatic alarm.   A fire, later described by the Firemaster as one of the most operationally difficult and serious fires of that year had taken hold in the double basement floors.   On street level no flames or even smoke was visible and the lights were still on in the foyer.   Hose pipes straddled the road which was awash.   The person in command instructed that foam be pumped into the basements as there was fear of an explosion.   A long night was anticipated, and I have a recollection of a coffee stall staffed by the W.R.V.S. or Salvation Army where yellow helmeted men grabbed a hot drink before returning to their exhausting and dangerous work in the dense smoke and intense heat.   It was an eerie, almost surreal sight with the continual steady hum of generators. Suddenly it all changed.   Voices were raised and men ran in various directions in quick response to urgent orders.   A fireman was lost.   Somewhere in the foam, and in the total darkness, he had fallen through a floor. He had not been found by the time we were relieved of our duties, but the next day we learned that he had been killed (for the purposes of this book, I made enquiries and learned that he was sub officer Archibald McLay). Ten other officers and men required hospital treatment that night and it was not until 12.30 pm the following day that the Firemaster was able to say that the fire was under control.   As a frequent attender at the Theatre Royal, I always think of that fireman and his brave counterparts.

Ma'am was a very ambitious woman with little understanding of anyone satisfied in a job they enjoyed doing to the best of their ability.   She felt that everyone should want to get to the top.   One day she challenged me "You obviously enjoy this plain clothes work, but have you ever thought what you will do when you are too old to be a teeny bopper".   Without hesitation, I replied "I'll just be an old hag".

She dismissed me with disdain.   I was a lost cause.

Police examinations which could be sat after two years service, were split into two – the Elementary and the Advanced and each had two sections – a general knowledge section and a criminal law, evidence and procedure section.   At the time I did not want to become a woman detective as they dealt mainly with indecencies involving women and children and this did not appeal to me at all.   As it was deemed necessary to possess an elementary certificate before being considered for the C.I.D., I decided I would sit the examination and pass the police duties to show I was keen and fail the general knowledge.   However, it backfired on me.   I couldn't believe when I learned I had passed the general knowledge for which I did no studying at all, and failed the police duties into which I had placed all my efforts.   I can only assume it was examinationitis from which I suffer badly.

I was completely laid back at the general knowledge not intending to pass, but was my usual nervous wreck at the police duties. The next year I passed the police duties section.

I displeased ma'am on another occasion when I was out with one of the squads and was instructed to tell no-one of the impending operation. On returning to the office following the briefing, ma'am asked me about it. I politely informed her that I had been told not to discuss it. The lady was not at all pleased, and I referred her to the head of the particular department. I don't know what transpired, but she made no further mention of it. On quite a few of the plain clothes jobs, I had worked with a Detective Inspector known as "The Flea", and it was he who approached me one day to tell me that a new department was being created to be called "The Scottish Crime Squad", and applications were being invited. He felt I should apply and offered to assist me to complete the application form. During my tea break, I called in at the adjacent drugs squad office where Jack helped me to compose my C.V. I didn't want anyone to know of my intentions as I was quite certain that I was sadly lacking in C.I.D. experience, and would fail to even get an interview because I had no examination certificate (ticket). When I returned to the policewoman's department, to my surprise the Sergeant who was from "B" shift and covering for my own Sergeant marched me into her room, slammed the door and demanded an explanation as to why I had "sneaked" into the drugs squad office to be with one of their officers. I refused to tell her and she continued her tirade that she was concerned about me as she was responsible for my moral welfare. I was ordered to remain in her room while she interviewed Jack who also refused to comment, respecting my confidence. The whole episode was ridiculous but was reported to my Inspector.   In private, I explained the situation and my certainty of failure being the reason for my secrecy. Miss Hunter repeated that most of us girls were young and vulnerable and the Sergeant only worried that I had been alone with this Inspector for some time.   The matter had erupted so quickly I had completely forgotten a crucial factor.   John, the Detective Sergeant in the squad, had been sitting quietly at his desk throughout my "clandestine" meeting.   Inspector Hunter then considered the matter closed and assured me of her confidentiality.   As a postscript, years later when Mairi and I were in a car being driven by a married cop on our way to a party, he stopped off at the policewoman's department to pick up "a friend".   It was dark, but I could sense the Sergeant's embarrassment when she climbed into the passenger seat, gave him a peck on the cheek, and then realised who was sitting in the back seat.

To my complete surprise, I was asked to attend an interview at the Scottish Crime Squad headquarters in Airdrie.   Jack told me that he had spoken with the second in command and had put in a good word for me.   I was thrilled and was up bright and early on the morning of my interview, only to find that my trusty A40 for the first time in its life, wouldn't start.   I was panic stricken.   I ran to our local station, where I got a train to Glasgow Central and ran to Queen Street station only to find it was impossible to get there on time.   I then ran to the taxi rank and en route to Airdrie explained my tale of woe.   The taxi driver was fantastic and told me to sit back and relax.   Precisely on time, he drove through the imposing gates and up the red chip driveway, stopping at the front door.   (I later learned that I had been the talking point as no-one, not the boss nor visiting dignitaries ever used the front door).   The butterflies were having a wonderful time in my stomach as I was shown almost immediately into the Commander's room.   He indicated a seat, introduced himself and nodded in the direction of the second in command "and I believe you know Mr Duncan?"

Without a glimmer of recognition I stared at the white haired gentleman smiling at me "eh, no".   I then realised that this was the ally, Jack had spoken of.   "Oh yes, yes, of course I do".

I was quite certain after that performance that I had definitely blown it, and was therefore floating on air when I was told I had the job.

Ma'am gave me a little talk on the perils of working with men and wished me luck.

CHAPTER NINETEEN

SCOTTISH CRIME SQUAD

The date was 17 November 1969, and I was a Detective Constable about to begin one of the happiest, exciting and most interesting times of my career.

A newspaper article of the time describes the Scottish Crime Squad as "Scotland's Barlow's boys", led by war time hero and former Chief Constable, Commander Bob Gordon.   In our first year apparently we solved 4 murders, 2 attempt murders, recovered stolen goods amounting to £36,083, traced 487 criminals and solved 426 crimes.   The article continues to describe us as "the shadows in touch with crime and the criminals" and "the faceless men".

There were about 70 male detectives, a woman Detective Sergeant and two women Detective Constables. Our secondment was initially for two years with an extension for a third year and if really lucky a fourth year.   Our mandate was to supplement Scottish forces in the investigation of serious crime and to collate crime intelligence.   Our own force warrant cards (identification) were replaced by a maroon coloured Scottish Crime Squad warrant card, identifying us in all parts of the country.   There were four other offices based throughout Scotland and on occasions personnel were exchanged to assist in an operation, giving added protection against possible recognition.   A tie was created which featured a scarlet pimpernel flower which was thought appropriate.

Almost six weeks after I began working in the Squad, one of the blackest days in the history of the City of Glasgow Police occurred.

On 30 December 1969, an armed robbery had taken place at the Clydesdale Bank in Linwood. Three men were involved. A short while later, Inspector Andy Hyslop emerged in a panda car from the rear entrance of Craigie Street police office, along with Constable John Sellars. He saw Howard Wilson and two other men carrying two suitcases and a heavy metal box into the close at No. 51 Allison Street, almost opposite the office, where Wilson had a flat. Wilson was an ex City of Glasgow Police Constable, having served ten years, and Andy knew him to speak to. His suspicions were aroused, and he left John Sellars in the back court while he returned to the office for assistance. Acting Detective Constable Angus McKenzie and Constable Eddie Barnett then accompanied him. They met Wilson in the street outside his flat and exchanged pleasantries. Andy Hyslop then enquired about the suitcases and tin box. Wilson denied all knowledge and readily agreed to allow the four police officers into his home. There in the living room, they discovered the two other men and the suitcases. The suitcases were found to contain canvas bags with money in notes and coins, the obvious proceeds of the earlier bank robbery. Andy Hyslop and John Sellars then left the room to look for the tin box. When Andy stepped back into the hall, he found Wilson standing a few feet from him with a gun which he raised, pointed at Andy's head and pulled the trigger. The gun clicked. It had jammed. Wilson then cleared it and fired again. Andy collapsed, bleeding profusely from a wound to the side of his face.   On hearing the shot, one of Wilson's accomplices fled from the flat.   Eddie Barnett ran into the hall and was shot in the head.   He died five days later.   Angus McKenzie was also shot in the head and shot again, as he lay helpless on the floor.   He died immediately.   John Sellars managed to radio for assistance while John Campbell struggled with Wilson for possession of the gun which he managed to do.   During this struggle, Wilson constantly asked his partner to assist him, but he did not.   John Campbell detained both men by means of the gun until two Sergeants arrived to assist.

Howard Wilson pled guilty and was sentenced on 13 February 1970 by Lord Justice Clerk, Lord Grant, to life imprisonment with a recommendation that he serve a minimum of 25 years.   The other two men were charged only with two bank robberies.   (They pled guilty to a previous bank robbery on 16 July 1969 at the British Linen Bank in Williamwood) and received 12 years imprisonment each.

I knew Howard Wilson as a colleague working at the uniform bar in the Central Division.

I also knew all the police officers involved, having worked at the Southern Division at Craigie Street.   Most of all, I knew Angus McKenzie.   He was married to June, the girl who had been my neighbour on my very first patrol.   He was a great guy who always had a smile and a twinkle in his eye.   I remember when he brought his new car to the office, and everyone had to go out to admire and sit in it.   We will never, ever understand the evil that possessed Howard Wilson to shoot in such a cold and calculating way, officers he knew and had worked with.

In the Scottish Crime Squad, we worked hard.   Initially we were paid a statutory eight hours overtime a week.   Occasionally we didn't do this amount, but more often we worked much longer hours.   On one operation in Edinburgh for example, we reported to Airdrie at 8.00 am to be through in Edinburgh for 9.00 am, finishing at around 11.00 pm, which meant I got home at 1.00 am to be up by 6.30 am.   This went on for some time as we elected to forego our days off until the end of the operation.

The Squad had many cars of all shapes and sizes. One however, bought in England was not a very good buy.   It was a lime green Hillman G.T. Reg. No. OCS999! Rather than being inconspicuous, we found the neds kept approaching just to admire it.

One job found us following a far superior car to anything we owned.   The target must have thought himself extremely unlucky that day.   As we sped down the motorway, we constantly had to radio ahead to different force areas, identify ourselves, and ask their motorway patrols to stop his car for speeding.   This was the only way we could keep up with him.   It worked perfectly until we reached the outskirts of London where a very uppity Metropolitan police controller instructed us to change our whisky call sign, as we were being confused with one of their cars with a similar call sign.   My protest to our Inspector that they should change, as we invented the stuff, naturally fell on deaf ears.

At that time, my knowledge of London was extremely limited and so I had no idea the next day why I was getting strange looks when I was left sitting in the car, while Ian and John went off on foot.   Eventually I spotted two cards in an adjacent shop window – "Fifi requires pupils" and "French lessons given".   I realised then, I was in Soho.

This operation was for crime intelligence purposes, Where was the subject visiting?, who was he visiting?, associating with? etc., and by the Saturday, enough information had been collated.   It was the Saturday of the Scotland/England game at Wembley and I finally got to see a football match.   The atmosphere was electric, although I was disappointed we were beaten.   I even got taken on to the edge of the hallowed turf.   After the match, we were invited along to a Scotland Yard function.   For the whole week, we had been surviving on chocolate bars from vending machines, and so John and I went to town on the feast before us.   It was only afterwards that our London counterparts told us that they were taking us out for a last meal.   As we sat studying the menu, our hosts told us "'ave anyfink you loik".   I chose lamb chops.   Not much eating on a chop I thought, but when six arrived, beautifully laid out, my heart ..... and my stomach ..... sank.

When we came home, we had a few days off.   On the Saturday, the Detective Inspector and I went to Hamilton race course to spot anybody worthy of note.   Next day, Ian told me when he'd gone home, his wife had asked him if he had a busy day.   Initially he had affirmed, but then added "well I was busy in the morning, but in the afternoon, Maureen and I went to the races just to see who was about.   "I know", replied his wife "you were on the television".

I had no knowledge of the intricacies of horseracing. On another visit to Hamilton I watched a particular man call at the bookies a couple of times to collect his winnings.   I followed him and saw him talking to a small fellow beside a fence.   When he returned to the bookies, I stood behind him, handed over my £1 and muttered "the same".   I then rejoined my colleagues who scoffed at my "no hoper" choice, but couldn't believe when it won.   When asked why I had chosen that horse, I told them what I had seen.   They were furious that I hadn't realised the significance and worse, that I had only invested a £1.

In Edinburgh, a ned's very fast car had been slightly doctored in an attempt to slow it down.   Imagine our feelings, as we sat and watched the local bobby and the ned with their heads under the bonnet. As we sat in our squad car, the D.I. muttered "I just hope for the sake of that cop's career prospects, that he's a lousy mechanic".

Whilst following this particular criminal along Princes Street, John decided to alter his appearance as he had been following him on foot.   He donned a headscarf which I kept in the glove compartment.   It was effective from a distance, but when we stopped at traffic lights, the headscarf and full beard attracted more than a few glances from pedestrians.

The next day I was following the subject on foot when he disappeared up a lane.   It was imperative to find out exactly where he was going as we suspected he had a lock up or safe place in the vicinity, and so I set off after him, message bag in one hand, and a chocolate biscuit in the other.   About half way up the lane, he disappeared into railway arch premises, but as I drew alongside, he re-appeared.   Our eyes met and so I smiled cheekily and proffered my kit kat …. "want a bit?"

"Aye, but no of the kit kat".

I tutted, giggled, and walked on ....if only he'd known.

A dubious business man in Glasgow was the proud possessor of a powerful sports car. We sat patiently watching his premises for hours. Eventually he came out, got into his car, roared up to the corner and turned right. When we reached the corner, we were just in time to see him turning left. When we reached that corner, he was gone. A morning wasted.

John and I spent a week on night shift in a small van. We covered the back with cardboard and with an old blanket would take turns of trying to sleep, but it was so cold. The regular postman I am certain thought we were a homeless couple.

Another old transit van was a favourite for observations. Bill and I suitably attired, were travelling down Buchanan Street. As we stopped at the traffic lights at Argyle Street, we spied a Rolls Royce with an elderly and obviously wealthy couple attempting to park outside Frasers store. Bill wound down the window and began to direct the driver, much to his wife's amusement. They parked successfully, the traffic lights changed, and as we moved off, the lady gave us a sweet smile, reserved I am certain for people she met, like us, while carrying out her good works, accompanied by a little wave, which I could have sworn was a Royal gesture. I am sure we would be the subject of conversation at a few dinner parties. In contrast, our old van was sent to the motor graveyard shortly after, when the hole on the floor on the passenger side began to expand to dangerous dimensions.

Observations can be tedious and none more so than an evening sitting in West Campbell Street. Finally, the vehicle we were waiting for appeared. Ian went to start the car ... nothing ... he tried again ... nothing. He was raging. I quickly radioed another vehicle to take over and then watched in disbelief as Ian in sheer frustration attempted to push our car and me up the hill.

Another uncomfortable night/early morning watch took place during an extremely cold winter spell. We could not run the car engine in case we flattened the battery. Alex brought along the biggest blanket I have ever seen. It tucked in from my left side over the gear stick and Alex and tucked in at his right side. It also went from our feet up to our necks. To make sure that the engine was still functioning, we would move our locus occasionally and this Alex mastered without even disturbing the blanket.

While we had a selection of cars to choose from, we also had a team car in crime intelligence. My Detective Sergeant was Willie, a most unlikely looking police officer. His looks are best described in the following story. He was walking up a close reading the name plates to ascertain which floor a particular ned stayed on. A wee lady opened her door, took one look at Willie and said "insurance money?" Quickly he replied "I'll get you on the way down hen". We then beat a hasty retreat.

Another example of Willie's incredible tenacity was a ned he began 'phoning. At first the ned was naturally suspicious, but eventually was confiding in Willie, believing him to be a fellow rogue. They never met, but would chat on the 'phone for ages.

Willie and I had a few small successes. We spotted a well known face looking in a T.V. shop window in Paisley. He then proceeded inside, but a few seconds later re-appeared carrying a television set. Willie followed him as I ran inside and verified with the staff that he had not been collecting a repair. The staff were astounded. The television was from their window display and they did not even recall the man walking into the shop. I joined Willie and he was apprehended.

A particular pub in the Paisley area was singled out as being a good source for stolen property via its customers. After a couple of nights watching the comings and goings, we were approached and Willie suggested that we would be interested in electrical items. The next day, as arranged, we met and followed a couple of neds in their car into a housing scheme. A price was agreed for the items and they were loaded into our car. Willie refused to hand over the cash until we were clear of the scheme supposedly in case we were hijacked. One of the neds accompanied us in our car and by prior arrangement we were stopped by the local C.I.D. The property in our car included a portable television, two record players, a tape recorder, two guitars and two transistor radios. All the property was later recovered except for £5 in cash, and one of the neds received 18 months imprisonment. Later while talking to my next door neighbour, she told me that her nephew's shop had been broken into, but the police had got all the property back. We were both quite tickled when I told her that I had been involved in the initial enquiry.

We had an 1100 motor car which we equipped with a telephone directory, sets of plastic cutlery for the many carry outs, a dog lead (great excuse for wandering down a lane), and a change of clothing. The girls in the squad had been allocated some money to purchase items useful for crime intelligence work. I always carried in my bag, a light raincoat, a wig, headscarf, pair of spectacles with plain glass and an engagement ring. The ring was slightly embarrassing, as young girls on a couple of occasions admired it and I had to keep my fingers firmly wrapped around the three "diamonds" in order to hide the tarnished "gold" band. I became an expert at changing from skirt to trousers and vice versa in that little car. We also devised our own form of signals. If the person on foot walked along the edge of the kerb, it meant they wanted picked up. Keeping to the inside of the pavement meant keep back. A fault I have often seen on television "stake outs", is where the two officers on observations carry on a lengthy conversation looking at each other ….. you talk to each other, but never, ever take your eyes off the locus.

I only had one road accident, but unfortunately it was with the flashy lime green Hillman G.T. I was taking it home with me (with permission). It was a frosty day and as I approached a set of traffic lights, they changed. The old wooden framed shooting brake in front of me stopped dead and I didn't. There was an ominous bang as I skidded into it. On inspection there wasn't a mark on the other car, but sod's law, unknown to any of us, our car had been in a previous accident and with every breath I drew, another piece of cataloy fell from the front of the squad's pride and joy. The other driver was quite satisfied, but I had to explain that as it was a police vehicle I was duty bound to report the accident. I remember my horror as the traffic Sergeant taking the report, kept picking more cataloy from the car.   I telephoned my Chief Inspector who was most understanding.

"Are you alright?"

"Yes"

"Is the car a write off?"

"No"

"Well, you're not even a member of the club.   Don't worry about it.   I'll see you in the morning".

The next day, I felt so bad when he gave me the accident report to complete that he sent Irene, my Sergeant, downstairs to check that I wasn't trying to commit suicide.

My accident was not nearly as dramatic as two of my colleagues a few weeks later who radioed in to report that they had collided with a boat.   The Commander, who happened to be in the office, was livid "where the hell are they?   They're supposed to be on the M73".   It transpired the boat was on a trailer.   Our team in this case was completely blameless and damage fortunately was slight.

I had one other near miss when Sheila and I were sent to a particular pub to witness a meeting between two criminals.   When we came out, and got into the mini, I checked my mirror, over my shoulder and began to do a "U" turn.   I heard a screech of brakes.   A car had obviously been at my blind spot.   I drew alongside and found myself apologising to the well known Scottish actor Roddy McMillan who very seriously said "that really wasn't very clever was it?"   I agreed, and we shot off.

Following someone either on foot or by car is not easy. They come in two categories.   If the follow is the result of a tip off that the subject is going to commit a crime, then it has to be close, not close enough to be spotted, but not too far away in case he is lost.   If the follow is for intelligence purposes, then it can be maintained at a distance.   If he is lost, then contact can usually be made again at his home, workplace, usual haunts or associates houses.

In the first category, a tip off was received that a robbery was to take place at a certain bank.   A car had been selected by them which was always parked in the morning in West Street/Scotland Street by the owner, who then caught the subway.   After a lot of deliberation it was decided by the bosses that the risk of injury was too great to the employees and customers of the bank to allow it to go ahead.   Also a follow would be necessary just in case the locus was wrong.   That created the possibility of losing the neds or of them realising they were being followed, when things could get nasty.   These were vicious criminals.   The decision had been made and we sat watching the car which was to be stolen. Word was passed to us that the team was on the move, and a follow at a discreet distance was maintained.   We watched as the three neds broke easily into the car and transferred a heavy bag into it from their own vehicle. We pounced and it was found to contain face masks and pick axe handles.

On another watch in the second category, Willie and I had followed a ned all over the city, noting his routes, places visited, etc.   He then drove northwards out of the city.   At this point we asked for assistance and a Detective Inspector responded.   He overtook us as the subject headed over the crest of a hill and down to a roundabout,

where he took a small road to the right.   As we watched
from the brow of the hill, Tommy missed the cut off.
Once on the right road we easily picked the target up
again, but the D.I. was not a happy puppy at losing the
ned after two minutes.

CHAPTER TWENTY

SCOTTISH CRIME SQUAD

I was despatched in the old van to an operation in Inverness.   I had to find my own accommodation and then rendezvous with a particular officer the next morning. Due to a conference in Inverness, I found it extremely difficult to find a room and eventually ended up in a "broom cupboard" with four wall hooks as a wardrobe. The wash hand basin extended over the end of my bed, and the toilet was at the end of the hall.   I placed both pillows down the centre of the bed which raised it to the same level as the sides, and folded my coat as a pillow. I was there for almost a week.   We worked during the day only, but the newly married officer was not interested in entertaining me in the evenings and I was left to my own devices, which included going to see the film "On the Buses" twice at the only cinema.   The working relationship with this officer was such that I can't even remember his name, but we agreed that he would drive as he knew the area.   I couldn't believe that we lost our target after fifteen minutes.   This can happen to anyone, but not when you stop at a zebra crossing and wave to an elderly lady to cross.   The next few days, I drove.   I was grateful when that job ended.

Sheila had a better time working in Fort William with a male colleague.   A very nice chap who rather fancied himself, and, possessed with typical male ego, had taken the usual action when finding himself follically challenged, of having a very low parting with long strands carefully combed and stuck over the encroaching bald patch. When the intelligence required had been obtained, they decided to go up on the ski lift, before heading back. As they sat side by side, Willie gazed at Sheila in true romantic Hollywood style. She struggled to keep a straight face. He thought she was looking at a handsome son of a bitch. She knew she was looking at a middle aged white face, sunken eyes, bright red nose complete with drip and the longest wisps of hair blowing carelessly in the wind in the opposite direction from his shining pate. Sheila returned his smile, secretly thinking "why do you never have a camera when you need one?"

After a long tedious operation watching a subject moving house, he and an associate helping with the flitting, drove off in their van as darkness fell, but this time, they left the Edinburgh streets behind and drove along narrow country roads. Occasionally we switched off our lights hoping to fool them into thinking we had turned off the road. Finally, they parked in a secluded car park. There was no way we could follow them, and it was a case of waiting patiently in the blackness listening for any sounds, and watching the vehicle. Minutes turned into an hour and then they returned. We pounced and found them with two large sized carpets. We discovered that a warehouse nearby had been broken into and a large selection of household goods were stacked, ready to be loaded into the van and transported to the new house.

Not so successful was a watch in Lanarkshire. A few days of nothing happening had dampened our enthusiasm, when, just as darkness fell and we were changing shifts, the subject appeared and drove off. The adrenalin began pumping as we all followed him through quiet villages and country roads. We could see the look of astonishment on the beat Constable's face in one village as first one car, then another, then another, and finally a motor bike bringing up the rear, passed him. I think it was more traffic than he'd seen all week. Finally, the subject stopped at a quiet junction and a second occupant climbed in. We were on a high. For sure this was it. In total blackness now, he drove up a quiet lane and the lights went out. We sat quietly, windows down, listening for car doors closing, footsteps, anything to indicate they were leaving the vehicle. Nothing. Two men were elected to creep up towards the car to find out what was going on. They returned a few minutes later. Our subject was having an extra marital affair and was far too pre-occupied to be interested in carrying out any criminal activity that night !!!

In Kirkcaldy, we watched as a professional team of shoplifters returned time after time to their vehicle with large quantities of stolen goods. They made frequent return visits to the car, so that, if caught in any of the shops, they were only in possession of items from that particular store. Again at the end of the day, their intention was that only the driver would return to Edinburgh by car, the others returning by bus. Therefore, if the vehicle was stopped, only one member of the team would be caught. They were devastated to be apprehended at the end of their busy, lucrative day.

At the end of some operations, the Edinburgh boys would take us along to the pub at the end of the road, where an exotic dancer performed. Normally no females were admitted, but an exception was made in the case of Irene, Sheila and I. We found it highly amusing. All the men were engrossed in conversation and the dancer found herself with an audience of three as she gave it her all. We felt quite sorry for her and were always the first to applaud as the strains of some top twenty hit faded out, which then prompted a half hearted response from the male clientele. We nicknamed her Miss Appendix 1970, as her brief bikini line outfit didn't quite cover the tell tale scar. She only seemed able to perform to the one record and on one occasion gave vent to some extremely strong oaths in a broad Edinburgh accent when the barman put on the reverse side by mistake.

On another occasion, I had been elected to drive Willie (1), John and Willie (2) back to the office. They had a few pints and when we set off, John and Willie (2) settled down in the back seat and promptly dozed off. However, the other Willie in the front passenger seat began to get a bit amorous, putting his arm around my shoulders and telling me what a wonderful person I was. I asked him several times to go to sleep to no avail. I then did something which I realise now was very dangerous. I checked my mirrors. There was nothing on the M8 at that time of the morning. It was a dry night. I braked hard. John and Willie slid slowly off the back seat on to the floor, mumbled and shook themselves before settling down again, but the other Willie, with a strangled "Oh Christ" vanished from view somewhere below the glove compartment. As I accelerated off again, he hesitantly re-appeared from the gloom, eyes like an owl. He then sat in a huff all the way back to Airdrie.

Working constantly with men makes you quickly realise that you cannot beat them in a head on clash. You have to be subtle. I was working with the team and we were staying overnight in Edinburgh. At the end of the day's work, I realised by their little innuendos that they had their evening's entertainment planned which did not include my presence. I suggested that if they didn't mind, I would telephone my girlfriend, and arrange to see her for the evening. I could sense their relief. That evening they insisted on sitting with me in the bar until Peri arrived. Peri is an attractive girl with a good figure and personality to match, who can really turn it on when required. By design we sat at the large bay window. It was a beautiful night when Peri drove up in her red Triumph Spitfire, with the hood down, her long blonde hair blowing in the breeze beneath a leather cowboy hat purchased on one of our many holidays together. As she screeched to a halt and jumped out, her shapely body came into view. The comments proved that our plan was working and they were mesmerised as she walked confidently over to our table. Suddenly, none of them were in a hurry to leave and they were devastated when she announced that we were off to a "bash" which was unfortunately invitation only. In fact, we went to her tennis club "do", but they never found out.

We sat and watched one house in the east end of Glasgow for days without sighting the subject. We had all given up believing that he was actually there, until the vehicle closest to the locus put out the call we had all been waiting for "subject on the move". As usual, another cup of coffee went out the window. Firstly he called at an associate's house and after a few minutes, the two of them emerged, in deep conversation. We soon left the shops and houses behind and I became a little apprehensive as I was in open ground with no cover or excuse to be there.   Suddenly they about turned and began walking towards me.   I was certain I had been rumbled and immediately turned down a lane which appeared on my right.   It was a dead end.   There was only one thing I could think of.   I stepped into the bushes and making certain that I was slightly visible, I squatted and relieved myself.   I heard them passing and laughing.   It was a bit dramatic, but it worked.   They hired a car and drove to Edinburgh and then into the north of England.   We alerted our English counterparts who took over the follow.   They were eventually caught doing a snatch at a supermarket.

After several hours on one watch, Sheila decided to pay a quick visit to a public toilet conveniently situated about 50 yards from their car.   She had just settled herself back in the car, when a man very furtively came out of the ladies' toilet and walked hurriedly past them. Charlie could hardly contain Sheila, especially when she went back into the toilets and discovered a hole bored through from the next cubicle and something "not very nice" on the floor.   She was incensed, especially as they could not leave the locus or break cover.   The pervert will never know how lucky he was.   To this day, if I ever use a public toilet, I always check the doors on either side.

Sometimes a little imagination was called for when following a target.   One officer found an electricity junction box useful.   He examined it, checked a fictitious number from a piece of paper, knocked each side very carefully, putting his ear to it and wrote on his scrap of paper. All this was scrutinised by a curious little lady returning home with her weekly shopping. When he could eventually proceed, he carefully and deliberately placed the paper in his pocket, and nodded to his audience before walking off.

Another Constable hopped on a bus. As the subject paid his fare and went upstairs, Ian realised he only had a few coppers in his pocket and not the foggiest idea of the bus' route or destination. Discreetly, he attempted to show the driver his "special" Scottish Crime Squad warrant card. The driver was not impressed and in a loud voice shouted "aye fine son, where are you going?"

"I don't know" replied Ian confidently.

"What dae ye mean, ye don't know?"

Quietly Ian attempted to explain that he was following someone. The driver was still unimpressed "aye fine" and waved his hand dismissively. Fortunately this whole episode went completely unnoticed by the target who was safely ensconced on the upper deck, but Ian received a few strange looks from the lower deck passengers.

Sometimes even ingenuity is not enough. On looking through binoculars at the window of a target's house, I found him looking back at me through his binoculars.

Bill had taken up observations from a 'phone box when the subject walked straight towards him, opened the door and told Bill he hoped we were getting a lot of overtime out of this job.

I was sitting in the car with Willie one day when the ned walked over to us. Hurriedly we hid our paraphernalia, and opened the window. His words took us by surprise. "I know you're private detectives for my wife.

You're harassing me. I've got your car number and I'm reporting you to the police". Willie apologised and we drove off.

Sometimes a little help from the public is much appreciated. The Queen was visiting Stirling University and we had information that a certain faction was going to cause trouble. My remit was to mingle with them as a student from Glasgow University lending my support. This was quite acceptable to them. When the leaders explained their plan of action, I then passed the information on to our officers and the Queen's scheduled route was altered accordingly. It was working well until at one venue, the T.V. cameras scanned the crowd, and the interviewer, whom I knew well, stood facing us. Suddenly our eyes met. I quickly moved behind a student. A few seconds later, I allowed myself another glance to find his eyes locked into mine. Very slowly he winked and then turned away.

In the next operation, a certain company took quite a risk. A large lorry was to be followed on the motorway. Obviously a motor car sitting on its tail for a long distance would have caused suspicion. Through a contact, one of our squad managed to borrow a breakdown truck. Operation pigeon! was going well until Charlie saw a very disconsolate driver in a lay-by standing by a lorry from the same firm as the breakdown truck. His eyes lit up as he saw Charlie approaching and he waved his arm in a "slow down" movement which quickly changed to the "V" sign as Charlie whizzed by him. Apparently he spent ages trying to determine who had been driving the truck that day. On returning to the office a dead pigeon was spotted lying on the road. As the Commander had named the operation, the call went out "who's going to tell the Commander one of his men is dead". As a footnote, the lorry reached its destination safely, and was not hijacked as the information had suggested.

Another unusual venue was a dental surgery. The dentist only had one set of keys which were returned to him as he arrived for morning surgery. The subject had been very quiet during night shifts, but on this particular night he left his house and made his way to his lock up followed hastily by our two officers. He drove round various loci, returning to his house a few hours later. It was then, our boys discovered that neither of them had the key. Luck was on their side, however, for as they were deciding what to do, a District Council Lighting vehicle came along. A quick identification and explanation resulted in them being raised up to the surgery window which fortunately was a little open. As the subject's windows looked out on to another street, no damage was done, and neither the dentist nor the hierarchy ever found out.

I found myself in Church on one occasion. It was the east end of the city and it was a wedding. It was suspected that an escaped prisoner from a jail in England might try and attend the ceremony. I was greeted by a look-alike from the Adams family, obviously carefully chosen to stand at the Church door because of his bouncer appearance. Not a smile crossed his face as he growled "bride or groom?" I chose groom and a pew at the back of the already small assembled group, which in actual fact was only about five rows from the front. One by one, a further assortment of broken noses, scars and tattoos appeared, but still not a smile, nor look of recognition even, passed between anyone. There wasn't even a conversation between the groom and best man. The bride appeared and received a brief nod from her intended. The Minister announced the first hymn and we all stood like a domino effect in reverse. All the mouths began to move, but the Minister and I sang a duet. I didn't know the second hymn and the Minister manfully sang a solo for four verses. The escapee was there, and was arrested as he left the Church.

A Church featured in another operation. We were given permission by the Minister to watch a house from the Church balcony. It was kept extremely confidential as there could have been objections from the Kirk Session or parishioners. As arranged, at the end of the evening, Bobby was returning the key to the Manse and commented that the organist had come in to practise but he had kept quiet up in the balcony. The Minister was puzzled. The organist was on holiday and no-one, apart from Bobby had a key. The mystery was never solved and Bobby was very reluctant to take up his watch again.

An added bonus on this operation was the habit by the local fish and chip shop of handing in their left overs to the police office when they closed the shop for the night. No need for sandwiches. We lived on a diet of chippie delicacies for the duration of the watch.

I sometimes wonder how our stomachs survived the diet of greasy carry outs at odd hours of the day and night usually preceded by hours of fasting. On a watch, one of the team was delegated to get the carry outs for both cars, but when he returned to our locus we were gone, the subject having left his house to go walk-about.

He waited around and on our return we wolfed into cold fish suppers. Fortunately our flasks had kept the coffee warm, but it wasn't the most appetising meal I have eaten.

One afternoon, after a sausage roll and a creamy trifle with a single half cherry on top, I was dispatched from the back of the van in Gordon Street, and began following our target down Buchanan Street. It was a nice afternoon and, as he meandered along Argyle Street, I began to feel unwell. By the time he reached Gallowgate and stood waiting for a bus, I was really unwell. As he boarded a bus, I managed to let my team know and then was violently sick. A little lady stopped and asked me if I wanted to go to her nearby flat for a seat and glass of water. I declined, as the policewoman's department was only a few hundred yards down the road, but have always thought how kind it was of her. A car later picked me up and took me home, and I was off work for a week with food poisoning. Since that day I have never touched one of those tasty looking trifles in the paper casing.

Certain people are not cut out for crime intelligence work and John was one of them. He was always immaculate and had a very clean cut image. In a transport café, he stood in his Pringle sweater and casual trousers and announced in his refined voice to the assistant "I am a lorry driver". Totally unimpressed she asked him if he wanted a mug or a cup of tea...........he chose the cup !!

CHAPTER TWENTY ONE

MURDERS AND TOUTS

We had a few "characters" in the squad.   Davie, a Sergeant, had us enthralled as he recalled when he had been on the police driving course driving on the M8.   Suddenly the bonnet of the car had shot up obscuring his vision, but he instantly remembered the position of traffic in front and behind and brought the vehicle safely to a halt on the hard shoulder.   Very impressive until Irene told me later that the story was true, but the instructor had been driving and Davie, like her, had been a passenger in the back seat.   She described Davie thus "he picks up a biro pen and it immediately becomes a Parker".

One day on arrival at the office we were sent home to pack an overnight bag.   On our return, we learned we were going to Aberdeen to assist the local force with a difficult murder.   We were split into two cars for the journey.   When we met up, Davie told us he had taken his team to an upmarket hotel for lunch and berated our Inspector for stopping at a transport café.   However, the true story soon emerged that they had indeed stopped at this hotel but on seeing the prices, called in at a greasy Joe's café instead.   That was Davie.   As his team were unpacking, a porter arrived with two glasses of whisky "Your boss sent these.   I have to charge it to his account".   As quick as a flash Louis asked "Are these singles?".   The porter affirmed.   "I'm sorry, but our boss would be most annoyed.   He always buys us doubles".

The porter apologised, scurried off and returned a few

minutes later, having rectified the situation.   As Louis said later "if he wants to be a boss then he has to pay the price".

The murder victim was a prostitute by the name of Helen Wills and as her body had been found in Cumberland, officers from that force were also drafted in. It was the first time that English officers had worked alongside Scottish forces on a murder, resulting in another tie being created.   This time it featured two shaking hands. On one hand was the St Andrew's Cross and on the other the St George's Cross.

As Christmas approached, it was arranged for the English boys to go home on Christmas Eve to celebrate Christmas Day with their families, returning on Boxing Day, while we manned the office.   On Christmas Eve, we went to the midnight service in a local Church.   During carol singing, some drunken trouble making youths arrived, shouting and mocking the service.   Quietly our boys moved in behind and tapped them on the shoulder. As they swung round aggressively, they were confronted by five or so six footers.   A few quiet words whispered in their ears and they filed out without a murmur.   There were several grateful glances from the parishioners that night.

I remember sitting in the office the following day when someone asked what date it was .....25 December.   I felt very sorry for my mum.   I at least had company, but she spent the day alone with our unopened presents, much of our Christmas meal ending up in the bin.   In contrast, returning to our hotel that evening, the management had laid on a Christmas meal complete with crackers etc.   One of our single men had invited along a local, well endowed but not terribly intelligent young lady wearing an extremely low cut dress and, as was the fashion of the time, a watch pendant, which disappeared down her ample cleavage.   Each time she leant forward for a spoonful of soup, the officer opposite became an agitated wreck.   Finally he gave up trying to be discreet and allowed his eyes to remain transfixed.   At one point thinking she had noticed, he quickly commented "good heavens, is that the time already".   Totally unaware of the effect she was creating, she slowly retrieved the fortunate watch from its repose "aye, ten past ten" she replied innocently, allowing chain and watch to slowly slide back into the hidden depths, as the officer visibly drooled.

Another detective learned a salutary lesson.   He was boasting about a married "bird" he had picked up.   Her husband was a commercial traveller.   Sheila listened then quietly asked "I wonder what your wife is doing this evening?".   He looked puzzled "she's at home of course".

"That's what the commercial traveller thinks when he's away".

That officer's wife received a lot of evening telephone calls in the following weeks.

The same officer while entertaining the lady had romantically driven the C.I.D. car (which he shouldn't have had) on to the beach to watch the sunset, from where it refused to budge.   The lady walked home, while he pleaded with his colleagues to come and tow him out. Fortunately none of the bosses found out, but it cost him more than a few pints.

Hogmanay came along and it was the Scots turn for a

day off and also a chance to supplement our "overnight" bag.

In Aberdeen, it was quite a problem for our English counterparts to understand the broad dialect of some of the local worthies and on more than one occasion we were called in as interpreters.   I remember translating "ah wiz sittin ahin the dyke we some kwinies and loons" to a totally bewildered Cumberland officer.

Irene, Sheila and I collated all the paperwork and each morning one of us would attend the briefing held by Mr Huddart, the Superintendent.   When I returned to our office, Irene instructed me to stand in the middle of the room and give an account of the meeting.   Being a bit of a mimic, I began in my best Cumberland accent.   "At this present moment in time, we are 100% sure we've got the right man, boot we've got to prove it".   I expected more of a response from Irene and Sheila but when I turned in the direction of their gaze, I found Mr Huddart standing behind me "that sounds pretty accurate lass, carry on". I slunk back to my seat "I think that was it Sir".   Later he told me I was spot on with the accent.

Although there was a lot of banter, it actually was hard work.   We began about 9.00 am and finished only when it was convenient to halt a particular line of enquiry.   At the conclusion of the investigation after six weeks, with only one day off, our counterparts returned to England with a taste for stovies, baps and mealie puddens and we came home.   A man had been charged with the murder and was convicted, although some time later he was released due to uncertainty regarding the forensic evidence.

Another murder found us in Blairgowrie for about five

weeks, and it was here I first tasted venison. The Chief Inspector heard me praising the venison and salmon sandwiches provided by the hotel when we returned there in the evenings and told me he would hand in a package when I was going home on my rest days. I duly collected the polythene bag left at the office counter and my mum and I dined royally on the large quantity of venison separately packaged in neat little parcels. It was only when I returned to Blairgowrie that I found some very disappointed detectives who had all been expecting a little package to take home.

Again we worked diligently from 9.00 am with chip suppers for our evening meal and then back to the hotel for a pint and those delicious sandwiches. One night Irene decided to forego supper, wash her hair and have an early night. When we later went up to our rooms, I guided Bob, who was engrossed in conversation, towards our door. He didn't check the number, bade us goodnight and disappeared into the room. We waited giggling in anticipation – no reaction. I eventually went in to find him sitting on my bed quietly removing his shoes and socks believing that his room mate was already fast asleep. He shot off, socks and shoes in hand when I whispered it was Irene in the other bed. I also thought she was asleep until the door closed. The bedside light went on and this apparition with scrubbed face, cold cream and rollers sat bolt upright. She had been dozing when she heard someone coming in. She quickly realised it was not me when a deep gruff voice sighed "ah well" and burped loudly. She was not at all concerned about a man being in her bedroom as she was him seeing her in her night time attire.

The Blairgowrie murder was very difficult. A hotel owner was the victim and members of the berry picking fraternity were the chief suspects, but being a very close knit community mainly consisting of tinkers and having an inbuilt suspicion and hatred of police officers, it was impossible to penetrate the barriers. Officers told us of groups living in accommodation resembling hen huts and they had a language of their own. Detective Constable Johnston found out that the Johnston's were known as the Funkum's. "A femmin in the mun" meant "a slap in the face" and "a strode in the durabels" meant "a kick in a sore place!". Eventually the enquiry was wound down in numbers, unfortunately remaining unsolved.

Touts are a very important necessity, and have various reasons for supplying information. Some do it for the monetary reward, some for revenge, some for the feeling of importance and occasionally community spirit.

One Edinburgh lady, however, was in a class of her own. All her information proved fruitful, but it transpired that she was organising the crimes and then shopping the perpetrators, and her reason …..she had too many police officers to satisfy and not enough information !!!

She was a real police groupie, listening to police messages every night on her radio. She knew all the call signs, much to the embarrassment of one young police Constable. She was leaning out of her window and watched as he acknowledged a call for ZH23. "That's no ZH23 you're in son, that's ZH24"… and she was right.

One tout caused us concern when he went missing from all his usual haunts. When he finally contacted us he was quite indignant. He had gone down to Liverpool for a football match and got arrested for being drunk and disorderly.   On appearing at court the following morning, he found himself before a black magistrate who asked him where he was from.   When Willie replied "Glasgow", the magistrate commented "you're far travelled".   "Yer no exactly a local yersel" retorted Willie and promptly received thirty days imprisonment.

Another tout was rather unlucky.   He was to be the driver in a big housebreaking.   We were all standing by in the office when the Detective Constable got a 'phone call from his tout to say he had 'flu', was feeling awful and didn't think he could go on the job.   Depending on his information, Eric ordered him out of his sick bed and the housebreaking went ahead as planned, but the arrangement whereby the driver was to escape nearly didn't go according to plan.   As we sat in the office congratulating ourselves, the 'phone rang.   It was the tout.   He had been chased across snow covered January fields by an over zealous police Constable and had only escaped by slipping out of his jacket and hiding in the undergrowth, where he remained until he felt it was safe to move.   He had then trekked across the fields in his shirt and denims until he came to a road and a 'phone box.   He could hardly speak and Eric later told us when he picked him up in the car he thought the poor man was going to die.

When I joined the squad, a Detective Sergeant I had known from my days in the Southern Division, and now a Detective Superintendent gave me a present of a tout. He was passed his sell by date and was more than happy to receive second hand clothing in lieu of cash, but living in a particularly bad area of the city, he managed to come up with interesting little snippets of information. The only problem was, that in general, touts liked only to deal with one person and my neighbour at the time was not too keen on letting me disappear to some unknown location.   We then devised a plan whereby I put my tout's name and address in a sealed envelope which Sandy kept.   If I didn't return within a certain time he would then know where to come and "rescue" me.   Fortunately it never came to that.

Sandy and I were sent to a Chinese Restaurant for lunch one day to test the effectiveness of a new microphone in the form of a tie clip.   Back at the office we were astonished at the results.   It began with us taking our seats, then a soft whistling of the tune "The carnival is over" with my voice in the background talking as instructed, to test the capabilities of the equipment.   We ordered our meal, followed by my conversation being almost drowned out by the continuance of "The carnival is over".   At the conclusion of the meal, Sandy and the waiter had a short conversation followed by .....yes you've guessed it.

Neither Sandy nor I were aware of his whistling, but it took him a long time to live it down.   Whenever he walked into the room, everyone began to whistle his tune.

CHAPTER TWENTY TWO

UNDERCOVER

On a pouring, wet night, Bob and I were hiding in thick undergrowth hardly able to see our objective for mist …. A large secluded country house.   Bob had proudly shown me his new overshoes and was boasting about how dry and warm his feet were.   After a few miserable hours, we saw the headlights of a car in the driveway approaching the front of the house.   We strained and caught a glimpse of three occupants alighting from the car.   The door of the house opened and framed in the light of the hallway, we saw our subject.   We also saw a Labrador and a very large "something" run out excitedly on to the gravel driveway, where they immediately stopped dead in their tracks, noses in the air.   Barking they ran towards us.   I froze.   It was at this point that Bob decided to confess that he was terrified of dogs, particularly big, barking dogs, and off he disappeared into the black void.   The dogs stopped within feet of me, panting as they stared into the gloom, ignoring their owner's call.   On a second command, they hesitated, heads twitching, then ran back and disappeared into the house, along with the owner and the occupants of the car.   I waited for a few moments before retracing my steps.   I soon heard Bob's soft curses and found him in a ditch.   He squelched and slurped all the way back to the car, never once mentioning his mud filled overshoes.

Another large country mansion was of interest to us.   Information had been received that the owner had in his safe, the proceeds of a large robbery. Unfortunately when we arrived at the house armed with a Warrant to Search the premises, the owner was away for the day, leaving his very pleasant, co-operative sister in charge. She contacted him and over a cup of tea explained the rift which had developed between herself and her brother. In her opinion he had done well, but had forgotten his roots and had become "a toafee nosed bastard". She continued "it all came to a head when he and his poash pal came home wi a couple a lassies. He didnae even introduce me and wiz treatin me like a hired hand. Ah wiz that annoyed ah jist tellt them … maybe av goat nae fuckin culture but av goat mair fuckin manners than aw you whores an whoremaisters pit the gither ….. ahm telling ye he wisnae very pleased". I suggested that perhaps she had been a little over the top, but when he arrived back, I could understand what she meant. They had both been brought up in very humble surroundings in Govan, but he now had a most affected accent and condescending dismissive attitude. I was very disappointed when our search proved fruitless.

Kenny found himself in a tough Lanarkshire mining village with a remit to infiltrate and gain the confidence of a local team who drank in a particular pub. On the first few occasions, everything went according to plan and our vehicles sitting some way off in case of trouble were not required. Kenny was being accepted by the locals and more importantly by the gang we were interested in. We were becoming a bit blasé when, as usual, closing time arrived and customers began to leave the pub after their lunchtime drinking session. The pub doors closed, but there was no sign of Kenny. One car toured the area in case somehow we had missed him, and we sat watching. Our Airdrie base was informed so that a decision could be made as to whether we should gain access to the pub on some pretext. We waited anxiously until we received a call to return to the office …he had been picked up. There we found poor Kenny with his head down the toilet. Having been totally accepted by the gang, he was "invited" to stay on after closing time so that the "bevvying" could continue. His only slurred comment was "boy, can these guys drink!". He was driven home by the Detective Inspector who explained to his wife that it really was all in the line of duty. Later when a robbery occurred, the team was rounded up thanks to Kenny's intelligence.

Although I was in the Squad, I still enjoyed nights out with the girls in the Bier Keller in Glasgow. Of course we were never police officers. My pseudonyms ranged from a Welsh holidaymaker with a rendering of the longest village name in Wales, to a Spaniard living in Glasgow studying English. When I told them my name was Maria del Carmen Sanudo Gaspar Fernandez and threw in a few Spanish phrases from my night school lessons, nobody doubted me even with my fair hair and blue eyes. As a group we were also professional hand clappers backing singers with a 1-2 clap, a 2-1 clap, or even a 1-2-3 clap. One night two guys began talking to Jean, and I recognised them as a couple of local hoods involved in all sorts of nefarious activities. I told them I was a ground hostess with B.E.A. at Glasgow Airport working out the weight distribution on the aircraft. One began calling me Cuddles and asked if I could get him a good seat on the plane on his numerous visits to London.

Obviously this would be great intelligence and I agreed, hoping that the Squad would be able to organise something. However, it was not to be. While sitting with them one night, Jean spotted a policewoman sitting with her boyfriend who waved over to our companions. I followed her into the toilet and asked her not to mention our occupations to her boyfriend, to which she agreed. Later on, John suddenly asked me where I kept my baton. Of course we denied it, but it was obvious the damage had been done.

Probably the most dangerous case I have been involved in was a large scale money lending operation. Myself and an officer from the Dundee branch of the Scottish Crime Squad, along with my friend Mairi, who was at that time with the Flying Squad, and her partner George, on four occasions sat on a Friday night in one of the toughest pubs in Glasgow at that time, the Molls Mire Public House in Polmadie, and watched as money was taken in and paid out. These men were violent criminals, but we felt re-assured that our presence had been accepted when one of the subjects asked Pat, my neighbour if the two dolls were "goers". Mairi and I were even followed into the toilet by a drunken woman who dismissed me "you can huv ma son, but she's fur me". Mairi's face was a study as she stuttered "ahm wi a bloke hen".

Each Friday night at closing time, we would make our way to the Central Police Office and write up our notebooks as to who was present, who was collecting and who was paying out etc. When Pat got locked out of his hotel one night and no amount of 'phoning or banging the door would arouse the night porter, I telephoned my mum to say I was bringing a Dundee officer home for the night. We asked Tom, the elderly night shift civilian telephonist to put a message in the book explaining that we would be late coming in that morning and the circumstances surrounding Pat's accommodation. When we arrived at the office, we were greeted with winks and cheeky comments. Being directed to the message book, Tom had boldly written "Pat is sleeping with Maureen tonight. They will be late coming in, in the morning". Even the boss had a twinkle in his eye when he said good morning.

Twenty five officers were involved in the operation covering several pubs in and around Glasgow and twelve men were charged with illegal money lending, threatening borrowers with violence, assaulting four of the twelve named borrowers who gave evidence and one accused in addition charged with possessing 15 rounds of .22 ammunition.

The newspaper headlines of the time were quite dramatic too.

"Their place of business was a pub, their office a toilet" and "girl detective (me) tells of her vigil in city pub".
317 witnesses were called to give evidence and 150 productions shown to the jury. All 12 accused were on legal aid and the trial was thought to have cost in the region of £25,000. After a lengthy trial, 8 of the accused were found guilty of illegal money lending (by their own admission) and the other 4 had the charges of illegal money lending dropped. Even the charge against the one accused of possessing ammunition was withdrawn, and because the accused had been in custody for three months awaiting trial, they were all freed.

One of the men in the presence of his lawyer later

complained "I am being hounded by the police. Twice I have sat in the dock accused of murder and twice I have been freed. I know I am no angel and have been in a lot of trouble, but I've paid my penalties and I think that should be enough!".

Moves were afoot and every day when we arrived back at the office the notice board was scanned anxiously. Gossip was rife and men discussed where they wanted and where they did not want to be transferred which prompted Irene, Sheila and I to compile a sheet listing each officer's nightmare move. After the Commander had left for the evening, we pinned up our notice relishing the moans and groans of disbelief. Only when we discovered one officer passing on the information to our Glasgow office, did we retrieve and destroy the evidence. When the boys realised, we all had a good laugh, but a few days later the genuine list appeared and as expected I found, that after four great years, I was being transferred to the Company Fraud Squad.

I left with a sad heart, a tie proving I had been a member of the elite Scottish Crime Squad, another commemorating the first time a Scottish and English force had worked together on a murder enquiry, and one from the pub where I held my last night party.

My time with the Scottish Crime Squad can never be repeated. It is now a highly sophisticated and far more advanced unit, but it is nice to know that I was there at its inception over thirty years ago.

CHAPTER TWENTY THREE

COMPANY FRAUD SQUAD

After the freedom of the Scottish Crime Squad, I must admit to being a little apprehensive on taking up my new duties.   The Company Fraud Squad was initially situated in the old policewoman's department within the Central Divisional Office in Turnbull Street, Glasgow. A Detective Chief Inspector was in charge with a Detective Inspector, a Detective Sergeant, and an assortment of Detective Constables, including latterly three women Detective Constables. I soon settled in and found them to be a good natured, helpful team.

The first duty of a new start involved contacting Company Directors who had failed to submit their Annual Returns and Accounts to the Companies Office in Edinburgh.   I soon realised that the type of person I was dealing with was completely different from the usual Crime Squad clientele.

A well known personality who was extremely rude dismissed me thus "I don't have time for all this.   Just you 'phone my accountant dear".   I took great pleasure in explaining that it was his duty to contact his accountant and failure to submit the required Returns within a week would result in him being asked to attend at our office to face charges.   His mood then became quite aggressive and I had to add that his failure to attend at our office if required, would result in a call being made to his place of business or at his home.   By this time his blood pressure was reaching dangerous levels.   He was no longer referring to me as dear and at one point in his very highland accent asked me to speak English. I concluded by advising him that if necessary a warrant could be granted for his arrest, but I was certain that a 'phone call from him to his accountant would settle the matter amicably. Although he slammed the 'phone down, his Returns were submitted within the week.

During Christmas week, Jean, also a new start, and I called at a city centre office to charge the Director with failure to submit the required Annual Returns. We found the office door open but in semi darkness. Coughing discreetly, we called out, announcing our presence to no avail. We then walked down a short corridor with doors on each side until we spotted a light in one of the rooms and pushed open the door to find a couple in a passionate embrace. A very embarrassed secretary quickly left as we identified ourselves and ascertained the Director's particulars. He explained that the office party had been that afternoon and the last person leaving had been instructed to lock the door. Having been charged, he cleared his throat a few times before confessing to being a good friend of one of our colleagues and suggesting that our discretion would be very much appreciated. Although we often had a giggle about it, we kept his secret.

In March 1974, I began working with a Detective Sergeant on one of the most bizarre cases to come to our attention.

Information was received from an ex employee of Rotary Tools, whose premises were in Brown Street, Glasgow, to the effect that bribes were being paid to people in various companies in return for orders.

Another ex employee living in England was named as being able to corroborate this information and a local police force sent officers to interview the man. Unfortunately as they advised him of the purpose of their call, a present employee of the company visiting the man, overheard their conversation and immediately advised the Managing Director of the police interest. He then took evasive action which included doctoring the filing system and disposing of sackfuls of paperwork. Apparently each index card in the office system had a small mark in the corner indicating that an employee of that firm was being bribed but by the time the police moved in, all cards had been similarly marked, making our task much more difficult.

Mr. Cochrane, the Managing Director was an ex labourer, actor, and deep sea fisherman, but was a devious, eccentric businessman. His office was decorated with zebra patterned wallpaper and spears and a stuffed elephant called Ellie sat in a corner. Prospective and present employees were occasionally instructed to sit on her. Witnesses also spoke of his office having a hidden tape recorder and small idol named Bung Ho, whose eyes lit up when an employee being interviewed supposedly told a lie. Both were of course operated by hidden switches on Mr C's desk.

Even a party to celebrate the opening of the premises was unconventional. A few days before the event, it was realised that the 1200 tickets issued actually admitted two people. As the premises were too small to accommodate this number, workmen were called in to demolish a wall and a marquee was erected. After the party, the wall was then rebuilt. Drink was apparently plenti-

ful but there were insufficient glasses, and a jazz band
and Iranian belly dancers entertained guests. A beauty
contest was held with various donated prizes, but prior
to the commencement, the judges were instructed that
Mr. Cochrane's secretary, a pretty girl, was to be the
winner.   Caroline, a very efficient and loyal secretary
later married Cochrane.   On one occasion she issued
a memo to the effect that as it was J.C.'s birthday (he
liked to be known as J.C. – Jesus Christ), 50p would
be deducted from each person's wages for a birthday
present.   Other biblical references prevailed.   The
premises were referred to as The Church, the salesmen
were Disciples and the order book was the Bible.   More
sinister was the bung book.

I began the enquiry having little sympathy for the many
people we interviewed who accepted inducements, but I
changed my opinion as the investigation progressed.

One storekeeper having been with his company for 18
years found himself unemployed after succumbing to
Cochrane's inducements.

Another gentleman greeted us in a friendly helpful
manner when we identified ourselves, but in a private
office I watched as this pathetic individual visibly crumpled before our eyes when he realised it was futile to
deny the allegations we were putting before him.   In
exchange for a favourable order/orders, he had been
provided with a free room in a top class hotel and the
services of a young lady.   He was near to tears as he
realised that because of this stupid act, he would lose
his job and the respect of his wife and daughters.   His
parting words to us were "I know it's no excuse, but I just
thought when I saw the girl ...when would a man like me

be able to have a woman like that".

Cochrane believed that every man had his price and gave out boxes of cigars containing amounts of money ranging from £50 - £3,000.   Presents included a television, music centre, cassette recorder, fridge, fishing equipment and a holiday.   These inducements resulted in fictitious repairs being carried out on existing tools, invoices passed for payment amounting to over £18,000 without any check that the goods had been ordered or delivered, an order for two pieces of equipment at a cost of £1,196 being increased to 14 items with an invoice for £8,375, and another order for 1 saw and 6 blades being increased to 10 saws and 60 blades increasing the invoice from £410 to £4,124.   When one company examined their tool store, they found they had enough stock to last them for years.

Many difficulties arose in this enquiry and none more so than in one large company.   The Director informed us that it was a delicate matter but he would endeavour to check their stock room during the lunch break.   On calling back later he informed us that he had been spotted by the union representative and told in no uncertain terms that should he continue his examination of the stock room, there would be a strike.   He had no option but to comply and apologised to us.   It is interesting that this company is no longer in existence.

Apart from Cochrane's dominance over weak willed company employees, he treated some of his own staff in a despicable manner.   He would entice salesmen from other employment with promises of increased wages but after only a few weeks would sack perhaps five out of the six, believing that if you fired a few people, the others could be ruled through fear.   He also believed that if an employee was subjected to "hate" treatment one day and "love" treatment the next, he would work harder in order to get more of the "love" treatment.

The three "ladies" who entertained corrupt company employees were very different in character.   One of foreign descent had the appropriate surname of "Grunt", pronounced as she kept telling me "Groont".   While in hospital years later, I heard a familiar demanding voice behind a screen.   The patient was being extremely awkward and rather obnoxious, until I was able to leave my bed and introduce myself quietly.   Her attitude immediately changed and for the rest of her hospitalisation she became an almost model patient.

The other girl regretted her actions, had since married and thereafter moved abroad.

The third was a rather shadowy figure who lived in a very well appointed flat with expensive décor.   Her taste in music appeared to be Tchaikovsky and Mozart and her book shelf contained "War and Peace" and "A History of the Law of Scotland!".   After giving evidence she left the court via a back entrance.

The Detective Sergeant and I travelled extensively throughout Scotland and as far afield as London, Birmingham, Leeds and Manchester interviewing over 100 witnesses.

On checking into one small pre-booked hotel near London, the elderly female receptionist consulted the register.   Without raising her head, she looked over the top of her spectacles.   She chose her words carefully and deliberately with emphasis on those she deemed important "MISS Ingram YOU are upstairs" indicat-

ing with her pen.   "Mr Rogers (pause) YOU are in the
ANNEXE", again indicating with her pen somewhere
beyond the front door.   As she handed over the keys, a
sniff concluded the transaction and she engrossed herself in some imaginary paperwork.

In Birmingham we stood at a long busy reception
desk.   The D.S. asked for two single rooms.   The receptionist consulted the register and then in a loud voice
announced "we only have a double room".   Slowly D.S.
Rogers turned to face me "well?".   Typewriters became
silent, fingers hovering above the keys, 'phones ceased
ringing, and conversations halted midsentence.   In
that moment, life on earth stopped.   "That won't do"
I whispered, shaking my head, consumed with embarrassment.   The typewriters resumed their incessant
chattering, 'phones once again demanded attention and
conversation filled the air.   The D.S. declined apologeti-
cally and we left.   In the car his laughter and recollection of the incident drowned out my threats to kill him.
Secretly I was annoyed at myself.   Had I thought quickly
enough, I could so easily have turned the tables.   He was
a deeply religious man devoted to his wife, whom I had
met on several occasions, and to his children, and would
have been horrified had I agreed.

Although the enquiry began in March 1974 and the
three directors of the company were suspended in June
1974, such was the complexity of the case, it was not
until October 1975 that the Managing Director and
Sales Director were charged with 16 offences of fraud
and attempted fraud.

The trial which lasted for five weeks, did have the odd
lighter moment.   An elderly man stood seriously in the

witness box extolling the virtues of Cochrane, but rather spoiled it when on leaving the court asked an official in a loud voice "where is Mr. Cochrane anyway. I don't see him here".

At its conclusion, Cochrane faced 10 charges, the others being dropped, and his Sales Director faced only 2 charges.

On 5th June 1976, headlines in the tabloids read "The party's over". Cochrane received a sentence of 1 year imprisonment and a fine of £650. His Sales Director was acquitted. The sentence seemed rather trivial considering the number of lives ruined albeit by their own volition.

It looked as though his bizarre behaviour was going to continue when we heard of his intention on release to ride an "Ellie" the elephant down the street from the gates of the prison, but to my knowledge this never materialised and like the rest of the characters involved he disappeared into anonymity.

Although I had no children of my own, somewhere there must have been a maternal look. When Jean and I called at the house of a Pakistani Company Director, we found ourselves in the middle of a family gathering. The baby who seemed to be the centre of the festivities was handed over to my care while its father gave Jean his attention. Meantime the infant gurgled and smiled much to the oohs and aahs of the assembled company. Jean appealed for some hush and valiantly began to read the charge, stopping occasionally to ask the besotted, completely disinterested father if he understood and to appeal again for calm. Eventually I was able to hand back my responsibility and we made our escape as the party resumed.

When a black woman was required to accompany us to the office, I ended up in her husband's car literally holding the baby as he followed the C.I.D. car. Bearing in mind this was the 1970's I found it quite a revelation each time we stopped as curious pedestrians looked at the Nigerian driver, then at my fair hair and complexion and finally at the gorgeous very black faced baby sitting quite happily on my knee. I wondered what my neighbours would think if they happened to spot me.

Again, as in all departments, there was the inevitable "polis" humour. It was well before the days of no smoking in offices, but Jim obviously had foresight and prepared an order supposedly signed by the Chief Constable, stating that smoking was prohibited in offices. There was only one smoker in our office and for a couple of weeks he dutifully stood outside in the corridor until conversation with other smokers made him realise no-one else was aware of this order.

Jean had been on holiday in Cyprus and brought back a bottle of wine for us to taste. Jim carefully decanted it and replaced the contents with water and vinegar. At the end of the day he then made a great show of opening the bottle. We all pretended to sip while watching Jean. She swallowed and her lips curled. "That's awful, it's vinegar". With a straight face, Jim suggested that perhaps it didn't travel well. Eventually he produced the genuine article which was very nice.

In 1975, a lot of changes took place.

The City of Glasgow Police ceased to exist and became Strathclyde Police, combining six forces, forming a very large and diverse area.

The policewoman's department was disbanded in preparation for the introduction of the Sex Discrimination Act 1975, all policewomen being integrated into the general pattern of policing and spread throughout the divisions.

Our Fraud Squad moved into the St. Andrews Square premises vacated by the policewoman's department and I appeared in the new Strathclyde Police Information Bulletin as one of the 270 policewomen carrying out every police task except for some reason, dog handling. I had been a member of the police rifle club for some years and latterly a member of the pistol club and a rather unflattering photograph of me with my gun appeared under the heading "have gun will travel". Two other photographs taken at the time had been deemed "suggestive" by the Chief Constable due to the way I was holding the weapon and banned from the magazine.

At the time, I was also working with the Flying Squad when required and another embarrassing article appeared in the Sunday Post entitled "The girl who daren't show her face – in case the fly boys recognise her". I received a lot of good natured ribbing and wisecracks over that.

After a short time, the Fraud Squad was again on the move to the new Strathclyde Police Headquarters in Pitt Street and it was from there that I was offered the chance to join the newly formed Serious Crime Squad which was to replace the Flying Squad.

Thinking it would be a repeat of my duties in the Scottish Crime Squad, I jumped at the opportunity.

HOW WRONG I WAS.

CHAPTER TWENTY FOUR

THE SERIOUS CRIME SQUAD

On 18th August 1975, I began the unhappiest time of my career. Of course I didn't realise that as I arrived at the newly renovated squad premises situated within Temple police office, near Anniesland Cross, Glasgow. I began about a week before the others and was given the task of typing out the teams of which there were three, one girl to each team. One of the Detective Inspectors whom I knew, on reading the list asked if I wanted to transfer to his team. I declined his offer as I had previously worked with Stevie on an odd occasion and believed he was a good Inspector to work for. That was my first and biggest mistake. He turned out to be the most petty, childish, devious and meanest police officer I have ever met in thirty years police service. It began well as detective officers over a morning coffee chatted to those they already knew and introduced themselves to those they didn't. The pleasantries didn't last long however. Out in the parking area, I climbed into the front passenger seat of our allocated squad car. This was a Scottish Crime Squad practice for the obvious reason that a couple in a car attract less attention when following a ned than two bulky police officers. Stevie stood with his hand on the door, a sullen expression on his face "that's the Detective Inspector's seat". I quickly apologised and moved into the back of the car. This became my regular position and only if I sat on the edge of the seat with my head stuck between Stevie and the

driver, like some inquisitive child, could I hear the conversation taking place.   I learned later from one of the
girls that she had been similarly treated and had given
up completely, spending her time reading a magazine.
On any enquiry, Stevie would take the male officer, leaving me sitting in the car.   It became extremely frustrat-
ing, and I don't think it would be tolerated now, but in
the 1970's it was useless to complain.   It wasn't only the
girls who were singled out.   One Detective Constable
was instructed to stop the car.   His Inspector and Sergeant then alighted, stood at the kerbside having a dis-
cussion before re-entering and ordering him to proceed.
This same officer spent most of one shift getting back to
the office by bus when his team ignored his radio calls
to pick him up at the Sheriff Court where he had been
giving evidence.

There was no camaraderie between teams, who worked
completely independently of each other, all the time
hoping to gain "brownie" points.   Such was the ambitious "look at me boss, ain't I wonderful" attitude that
on one occasion when the Southern Division requested
assistance, two cars were dispatched.   We followed the
Inspector into the Superintendent's room at the South
to be briefed on the enquiry, only to find one of our
younger officers already sitting there, having gleaned
all the information.   This man was a perfect example of
the "look at me boss" syndrome, but on saying that he
now holds a very high ranking position in Police Headquarters.

Following a robbery at a post office in Forge Street, the
armed perpetrators were known to be hiding in a block
of flats in Coll Place.   It was a painstaking, lengthy oper-

ation to trace and isolate them.   A gun was found in the bushes close by, having been discarded by the robbers, but it was not known for certain how many weapons had been involved.   Unknown to the police, the three men were listening to radio broadcasts and on hearing that police marksmen had been deployed, two of them left their hideout and gave themselves up to the Constable on the landing.   As officers of the support unit entered the flat, the third man also surrendered.   As the press gathered outside, little did they know of the chaos in the foyer as crime squad officers jockeyed for position to lead the neds from the building to the car.   I remember instructing one of the uniformed men to hang on to the cuff of the ned he had helped to arrest, little knowing then that years later that same officer would become my husband.

One is constantly amazed at the ingenuity of some neds and an unsuspecting member of the public became a victim of just that when he called at a toilet on the north side of the city.   He was asked if there was any toilet paper in his cubicle and when he affirmed he was requested to pass a few sheets under the gap at the floor.   On so doing, his wrist was seized and his watch removed.   By the time the poor man pulled up his under-pants, fastened his trousers and emerged from the toilet, the thief along with the watch was long gone.

I was not long in the squad when I committed my next cardinal sin.   I had been a member of the pistol club for a few years and as a member of the Serious Crime Squad went down to the Oxford Street Training Centre Firearms range to qualify as an A.F.O. (authorised fire-arms officer).   As our team prepared for the afternoon shoot, I was totally unaware that Stevie <u>always</u> won the small kitty.   We shot in pairs.   At a given signal, we fired two shots from a standing position, two sitting and two prone.   In the second sequence we ran diagonally to cover, loaded the gun and fired two standing, two kneeling and two prone.   Finally we slowly approached a turning target shouting the command "armed police stop" before firing two shots on three separate occasions.   As the instructor counted our scores and congratulated me on winning, I could see the anger on Stevie's face.   His teeth clenched and he turned red as he began to argue that he had two shots in the one hole (near the centre of the target funnily enough), but the instructor was adamant.   I found it rather pathetic that a grown man, an Inspector, felt his masculinity threatened by being beaten by a woman and even worse was arguing over a kitty of £1.20!   He sulked for a few days and it was yet another nail in my coffin.

On one of the few occasions when there was only myself and another officer in the car, we followed a well known shoplifter around the streets of Glasgow.   As Graham drove, I sat in the hallowed Inspector's seat, noting each place at which the subject stopped.   Eventually he parked his vehicle, walked into a Sauchiehall Street store and removed a large box of expensive dresses from a showcase.   He was arrested, taken to the police office, charged and eventually released.   Due to various reasons, it was some time before he appeared at court.   The accused was represented by one of Glasgow's more eminent lawyers, whom I knew well from my days in the Fraud Squad.   In answer to one of his questions, I related from memory the various stops the accused had made.   With a friendly smile (something all witnesses should be wary of) he asked "and did he stop anywhere else?"

"Not to my knowledge".

"Are you certain?".

I asked to consult my notebook as some time had elapsed.

He asked the usual question "Were your notes written at the time?"

I affirmed and he agreed.

I immediately noticed that there had been another occasion when the accused had gone into office premises.   I apologised and told the court about the additional stop. Mr. Murray's eyes narrowed and the friendly smile disappeared "mmm! And do you know whose office premises are at this address?".   I confessed that I did not.

"Would it surprise you to know that these are my office premises and my client had an appointment with me that day".

Mr. Murray had of course been wanting to discredit our evidence that we had the accused under constant observation.   After the guilty verdict he approached me outside the court and asked if I had acted deliberately.   He didn't ever believe that I had done it in all innocence.

One cold winter's morning, I found myself standing at a bus stop on a busy main road near East Kilbride. This was as a result of some ladies in the area who had approached the wife of one of our Detective Sergeants with the story that when they had been waiting for their bus, a male had appeared at the window of a house exposing himself.   They could give no description of the person as the venetian blinds had been positioned so that only his lower half was visible.   The squad sat in the car on the opposite side of the road, while I stood at the bus stop in question.   After a freezing twenty minutes of alternatively looking at my watch, stamping my feet and rubbing my hands, I suddenly became aware of the venetian blinds being slowly raised and I could see a pair of red underpants around the person's ankles. I then found myself staring at a dangling, dancing "willie" being put through its paces.   As it began to respond to the attention, I signalled to the boys and we made our way to the house. We were admitted by a youth and it was quickly ascertained that he was wearing red underpants and that he was the sole occupant of the house apart from his father who was a night shift worker asleep in an upstairs bedroom.   I felt so sorry for this man who had the shock of being wakened by a police officer and then being told that his son had been exposing himself to the public.   The youth tried to say that he had removed his underclothing because he had a boil on his bottom, but it was a rather feeble excuse not even believed by his father.   On the way to the police office, one of the officers, in an attempt to break the embarrassing silence spoke sympathetically to the boy "look son, you've got a wee problem, but I'm sure with your parents' support, you can get it sorted out".   It didn't help and silence prevailed once again.   Later the boys told me they knew he was exposing himself when I began to stamp my feet faster and rub my hands rapidly! They also added that I was the only one who knew if it was a wee or a big problem he had !!!

For the third time in my life, I found myself at a football match, this time between Rangers and Celtic.   Mrs.

Thatcher, who was in Glasgow, had expressed an interest in seeing the game. However, the lady, I suspect realising how unpopular her visit would be, chose to appear in the director's box just as the Celtic team made their way on to the pitch for the second half. The supporters began to cheer, but spotting the Prime Minister, began booing, then realising that it appeared as though they were booing their team, began cheering again. Blissfully unaware that her blue suit and hat was adding insult to injury, the lady, having made her carefully orchestrated entrance stood with that fixed controlled smile, giving a royal wave, as Rangers fans laughed and Celtic fans cheered and booed in total confusion. She did, however, take the advice of her advisers and was spirited away about ten minutes before the final whistle.

On a quiet afternoon, of which there were many in the squad, it was the custom for each member of the team to take a turn of buying the coffee. We wondered where Stevie was taking us as we headed north out of the city centre. Driving into the car park of the police office at which he had previously worked, he greeted his ex colleagues and made coffee for us from their office supply. By this time I was beyond trying or caring, and when it came to my turn, we visited Headquarters canteen. He positioned himself at the back of the queue deciding he would also have a cake. When I reached the cashier, whom I knew well, I smiled "three coffees Marie". She looked puzzled "three Maureen?". I gazed with a "I will explain later" look and affirmed. She immediately realised something was afoot and we completed the transaction. As Stevie went to pass by, she smiled and told him the price of his coffee and cake. I may have won the battle, but I certainly did not win the war.

About this time, one of the girls transferred back to a division, and I was asked by our boss to approach the divisional girls to see if one of them would be interested in joining the squad. Such were the conditions prevailing, that I couldn't find one interested policewoman, and a Detective Constable was seconded …..another Mr. Chauvinist. One evening I listened as he told me how he had been taken on because the squad wasn't performing well and needed more people of his calibre, and how it had been realised that the girls were a waste of space. His ego took a severe battering when I threw caution to the winds and told him that as anyone would verify, a vast number of policewomen had been approached and turned down the position, and he in fact had been a last resort.

Approaching Christmas 1976, Stevie, Graham and I drove to a quiet side street on the north side of the city where I was once again left in the back seat of the car while the two of them supposedly went to visit a tout. I read my newspaper from cover to cover, then re-read it including the sports and racing sections. I had begun writing in my notebook the time I was left in the vehicle, and I began to amuse myself by calculating the hours in a day I actually worked. As darkness fell and street lights came on, I seriously considered calling for assistance as they had been absent for over two hours. I had no idea where they were. As I pondered, they returned and we drove in silence back to the office.

A few days later, I was called to the office of our comparatively new Chief Inspector whom I knew from my Scottish Crime Squad days. Stevie had apparently noticed my notebook activities and had reported to him that he thought I was keeping notes on the boys. It was the one and only time that, without realising, he had done me a favour. At last I was able for the first time to air my opinions of some of my colleagues and produced the notebook containing my harmless time wasting notes. Unknown to me, wheels were then set in motion which became obvious later.

Meantime though, nothing much changed. I drove home from nightshift to discover that I had inadvertently taken the car keys home with me. For some reason the spare set could not be found, and although there were personnel and available cars, I was instructed to return to the office with the keys. It was a long journey from Clarkston to Temple especially through the rush hour traffic.

Shortly before Christmas I was in the office on a late shift and 'phoned home as usual to check on my mum, who, having suffered two major heart attacks and several secondary illnesses, was not at all well. There was no reply. I waited half an hour and 'phoned again, but when there was still no reply, I telephoned Jeanette, my good friend and neighbour. She went across to my house and let herself in with the spare key. When I 'phoned back, her words echoed in my head and chilled me to the bone. "I think you had better come home right away. Your mum is not at all well. We are waiting for the Dr.". No-one in the office raised any objections, and I broke all speed limits getting home, where the Dr. told me she had suffered a stroke and they were waiting for an ambulance. For the next few days I juggled work and visits to the Homoeopathic Hospital in Great

Western Road, Glasgow and it was during a visit on 26th December that my mum passed away. The staff would not allow me to drive home and insisted I contact someone. Being only a short distance away, I gave them the office number. I can only say that God works in mysterious ways, for at the precise time the 'phone rang in the office, a detective officer with whom I had worked in the Fraud Squad walked into the office with his female partner and overheard the announcement. He immediately volunteered his services and drove me home in my car, while Margaret followed in the police car. He then 'phoned Liz, one of my girlfriends, who was on duty, but immediately arranged time off and came over to spend the night with me. I was very appreciative of all their kindness, especially when I returned to the office some time later. Although some of the nicer officers did express sincere sympathy, my own Sergeant callously suggested that it was really a blessing in disguise, as, if my mum had been a vegetable, how could I have coped with work and looking after her. As everyone knows, it is very difficult after the loss of a loved one to face work and even friends. Your emotions are on a knife edge, and I found myself retreating to the toilet as tears welled up. Years later, when I heard that this man had suffered a heart attack, I remembered his words to me. Stevie treated me as though I had the plague, and avoided any direct contact with me. However, his curiosity did get the better of him when Ian called me into the Inspector's room and closed the door. As he gently explained that he too was an only child who had lost his parents and could understand the sudden emptiness and loneliness I was feeling, there was a knock at the door and Stevie walked in.   Mumbling an apology he went to his desk and searched through some paperwork.   We sat silently. Eventually he extracted a piece of paper with an exaggerated motion.   As he walked slowly to the door studying the note, Ian asked "could you close the door behind you Stevie?" He then continued that if I needed any help or advice with the confusing paperwork and officialdom that needed attention or someone simply to talk to, then he was there.   I must admit as I left the room there were tears in my eyes for a different reason.   In contrast to Stevie, Ian was an Inspector with a genuine interest in the welfare of those below him.   I couldn't help feeling that things could have been so different had I been in his team, but now it was too late.   I hated the squad.

At the beginning of the New Year, the Chief Inspector instructed me to deliver a parcel personally to the Chief Superintendent at Headquarters.   It was rather an unusual duty, but it slowly became obvious, when he asked me if I was enjoying the squad and would I be asking for an extension.   Suffice to say that I gave him an honest answer, a very honest answer, and he then offered me a post in a division when it became available.

I found it rather ironic that I wanted to leave a department because I was not being allowed to work, but was a very happy officer when, a short time later, I received the news that I was being transferred to "D" Division.

CHAPTER TWENTY FIVE

"D" DIVISION

I was extremely nervous on that January day when I arrived to take up duty at Stewart Street Police Office. (Later "D" Divisional office was transferred to Baird Street).

Since the time I left uniform duties in the policewomen's department and began working in the C.I.D. in the Scottish Crime Squad, Fraud Squad and Serious Crime Squad, the City of Glasgow Police had become Strathclyde Police, the Policewomen's Department had ceased to exist and policewomen now carried out the same tasks as their male counterparts.   I had also lost a lot of confidence after my experience in the Serious Crime Squad. The C.I.D. clerk, who directed me to my desk held an important position.   He was usually an older uniform cop with lots of outdoor experience and was therefore able to deal with any initial enquiry and report of a crime from members of the public calling at the C.I.D. office.   Big John was not just big, he was massive.   A large head sat on even larger shoulders and his muscle bound arms ended in shovels.   A booming voice matched his dark, mad eyes set below black bushy eyebrows.   I was told he liked me when he bellowed after me one day "hey wee Mo, that wiggle is the sexiest bum in the office!".   The story went that when Big John had arrived at the North many years before, he had been allocated a particularly wild area.   He walked along the road noticing that all the walls were spray painted with the words "Danny rules O.K." Approaching a group of neds, he demanded to know which one was Danny. He then dragged the protesting individual into a back close, beat the living daylights out of him, brought him back to his pals with the words "from now on Big John rules O.K.?". "Aye O.K. big man" replied the neds in awe, and with typical ned mentality … admiration.

The Detective Constables room was very large and airy and a buzz of business prevailed. After initial introductions I was handed a pile of green coloured sheets entitled Crime Reports along with a few enquiry forms. Watching the others, I followed their example and put the enquiries into my top drawer, but I was at a complete loss as to what I was expected to do with the Crime Reports. I sat very quietly over a cup of tea astounded at the hive of industry unfolding before my eyes. It was arranged for those attending court that morning to be taken there in one of the two C.I.D. cars while their C.R.s were divided up between the rest of us for initial enquiry. C.R.s were also arranged into areas to make full use of the two vehicles. As I had no experience of day to day enquiries, a detective officer accompanied me on my calls. I was amazed that I was being included in everything and being treated as a colleague not as a woman. After a week, the Serious Crime Squad was a distant bad dream. I was dealing with thefts of and thefts from motor vehicles, housebreakings, robberies and serious assaults. I was busier than I had ever been in my life and enjoying every minute of it. In contrast to my previous colleagues, when I tentatively asked for help regarding the non urgent enquiries I had secreted in my drawer, I was given immediate assistance as to where

and how to obtain the information requested.   Like a
bad dream though, the Serious Crime Squad had a habit
of rearing its ugly head from time to time.   Brian came
back from Court one day telling me that a detective
officer in the Squad had warned him that I was not to be
trusted.   Fortunately, Brian and I had worked together
in the Scottish Crime Squad and he told this detective
officer in no uncertain terms that I was completely
trustworthy and in contrast, he had heard from several
detective officers of the bizarre behaviour of the Serious
Crime Squad.

After a short while at the North, we got a new Detective Chief Inspector, who turned out to be none other
than the Detective Sergeant I had known in the Southern
Division and who had gifted me my tout. He was a dedicated police officer whose life revolved around the police
service, so much so that he often forgot the basic things
in life.   He was going abroad on holiday and as was the
custom put up a bottle of whisky for the boys when they
finished their shift and left with everyone wishing him
a happy and well deserved holiday.   However, the next
morning he telephoned the office from the airport and
asked the C.I.D. clerk to look up his annual leave form
as he had forgotten to take with him a note of the name
and address of the apartments he was going to .... On
his return home two weeks later he was regaling us with
stories of the different "birds" he had met.   Seriously I
asked "do you know why women are called birds, Sir?".
After a few moments deliberation, he confessed that he
did not.

"Because they pick up worms".   There was a hush and
then a mass exodus of officers from the room as Norrie's

mouth opened and closed.

On another occasion he was giving a hands on demonstration to a young detective as to how to frisk someone. As another officer came into the room, he suddenly realised how odd his actions looked …. Exit one very embarrassed Chief Inspector.

That was one side of Norrie, but one year while Headquarters were carrying out a survey for statistical purposes, it was discovered that Norrie had dealt with more murder enquiries in our Division than the whole of Scotland combined.

It was at "D" Division that I gained first hand knowledge of a ned's mentality and realised that all too often the Courts and "do gooders" make the mistake of trying to understand them using their own moral values.   If we were caught committing a crime, our first concern would be the shame it would bring to those close to us.   Shame is not something a ned feels, neither is sentimentality.   His possessions have either been supplied by Social Services, stolen or bought in some underhand deal in a pub.   Therefore there is no sentimental value attached to his belongings, and a prison sentence, devastating to any of us, is merely an inconvenience to him, which he can later boast about rather than try and hide. He has a completely different outlook on life as shown in the following case.

A fifteen year old boy along with his pal, neither of whom had been in any kind of trouble with the police, were in one of the local parks when they were approached by three neds who demanded the boy's bike.   He refused and died of a single stab wound to his stomach.   The lack of concern or remorse shown by the perpetrators is evident in their replies when charged.

No. 1 replied "It was a carry on that went wrong".   No. 2 replied "It was just a mistake".   No. 3 replied "It was just a joke that backfired".

In another case, my first attempted murder, a 24 year old man whose pal had been stabbed in a city pub, gate crashed a party in Springburn.   About 3.00 am witnesses spoke of the stranger asking for someone to go with him to the hospital to find out if his pal was "deed or alive".   Nobody knew what he was talking about and tried to ignore him as he had a flick knife.   In the hallway of the house a 19 year old youth, not known to the stranger, had shouted a gang slogan.   This prompted the stranger to stab the youth in the neck shouting "that's you chibbed now".   He then stabbed him in the stomach saying "that's you stabbed as well".   The occupants of the house sent for an ambulance and as the injured youth was being carried out, the accused who had remained at the party commented, "Every time I go to a party I end up stabbing someone".   One of the girls wiped up the blood and the party continued.   It was some time later before the police became aware of the incident and the party had by that time broken up.   It was quite a task tracing and interviewing all the witnesses who, having been drunk, had difficulty remembering what had happened.   I was therefore quite delighted when at the High Court a jury found him guilty and Lord Kincraig sentenced him to 8 years imprisonment.

The detective Constable's room was open plan and on one occasion Ian had recovered property from a housebreaking.   The complainer was identifying some jewellery, one item of which had us all completely baffled.   It

was a small curved, patterned silver charm on a chain.
Ian, quite innocently, asked the man what it was. Quite
openly, in a very effeminate voice he replied "my friend
gave it to me, it's a horses hoof". To everyone's credit,
you could have heard a pin drop.

A homosexual, leaving the office one day, asked the
detective officer to remind him of his name in case he
had cause to contact him. "Detective Constable Pile",
he replied. The gay complainer smiled mischievously
"you'd think me of all people would remember a name
like that!".

Two couples enjoying an evening out at a Chinese restaurant were asked to change tables by the manager to
allow a party of six to occupy their table. A few minutes
later the sixsome suddenly left and one of the lady's realised that she had left her handbag at the previous table.
A quick search revealed that her handbag was gone and
the two husbands ran out and were successful in apprehending the youths in possession of the handbag. The
manager had already called the police and the uniform
men attended, closely followed by ourselves. After the
usual formalities at the office, the neds were released. It
was about a year later when one of the accused, who had
pled not guilty appeared at the District Court. It was
a very cramped court and the accused was conducting
his own defence. Suddenly he accused me of failing to
accept his complaint of assault. I told him I had no idea
what he was talking about and he continued "I told you
that the man assaulted me and you just said … so would
I if you had stolen my handbag". While I honestly did
not remember saying that and denied it, to this day I
have a sneaky feeling it could be true as it sounds very

much like something I would say.

A very interesting enquiry occurred one nightshift when we were called to a fire in an Indian Restaurant which was closed for the night.   A large crowd from the surrounding flats had gathered to watch the Fire Service tackle the blaze.   I began speaking to several people who spoke of an explosion and it initially looked as though gas cylinders at the rear of the premises had exploded, until one woman said that she had seen two figures carrying white bags going towards the restaurant.   It was dark and that was all she could tell us, but it was enough to arouse our suspicions.   About the same time, my neighbour who had been examining the area found a coat with burnt hair adhering to the collar area and a white polythene bag in the pocket.   We both continued searching and recovered a white plastic container smelling of petrol.   Our most important find, however, was a pair of badly burnt trousers with a yale key and some money in one of the pockets.   It was obvious that the person wearing them had been badly burned and we immediately contacted all the casualty departments in Glasgow.   Back at the office we received a telephone call from the Western Infirmary.   A nurse had seen a van driving up to the entrance in Church Street and a man helped out wearing only a shirt and a towel wrapped round the lower part of his body.   Leaving him sitting on the pavement screaming for help, the van drove off at high speed.   On examination of his serious wounds, he was immediately transferred to the Burns Unit at the Royal Infirmary where we were eventually allowed to see him.   During our initial and subsequent interviews with him bandaged from head to foot, he only ever muttered two words to us …. "Fuck off", but the evidence was overwhelming, even down to the yale key in the pocket of the trousers found at the locus fitting the door of his flat. His co-accused was never traced and the reason never became apparent. Obviously the crime had racial implications, but there were also suggestions of an intended fraudulent insurance claim which went horribly wrong. Whatever the reason, he was later convicted at the High Court and received a lengthy prison sentence.

At Christmas time, as in most offices, we had a party in the C.I.D. office. It was strictly controlled by our patriarch Norrie, who would at the commencement have a collection of officer's car keys so no-one, having consumed too many drinks, could drive home. If any girl remained seated for any length of time he would approach an officer with the instruction "away and give the girl a dance son", but two dances later, terrified that he could be the instigator of some illicit affair, he would sidle up to the dancing couple "that's enough now son, away and dance with someone else".

It was after one such party that I arrived home and discovered my gold bracelet missing. I was devastated as it had been a present from my mum. The nightshift scoured the office and passed on word to the early shift. I contacted the taxi company and searched the pathway at my house. While sitting with a girlfriend sadly going over events, I got a 'phone call from John. He had been grappling with a ned and as they landed on the floor, he saw something glint below a small filing drawer unit. "Stop" John yelled to the ned who froze momentarily, as he reached into the small space and withdrew my brace-let. The ned came back to life immediately "Aw naw, yer no gaun tae pin that oan me.   Ahv never seen it in ma life before".

On a late shift I was accompanied by the Detective Sergeant who had recently come to our division and did not know the area.   He was a nice man but had a very gruff manner and was not enjoying the long walk along the drafty, dirty corridor giving access to the flats of Galloway Street.   Two young girls approached us with a rather dirty, neddy, Heinz mongrel plodding along behind.   I could see this canine watching Lyall who in turn had taken on the appearance of a bull terrier, his neck having disappeared, and in the place of cheeks there were two sagging jowls.   I swear I could hear the strains of High Noon drifting down from an open window high above us and as they got nearer and nearer to each other, their eyes locked.   Suddenly as they drew alongside the dog yelped.   "Keep that dug under control", snarled Lyall as we walked on.   I assumed without question that the neddy dug had gone for him recognising as neds do, even in plain clothes, that he was a police officer.   I was therefore completely gob smacked when Lyall announced "I knew that dug would go for me, so I got my foot in first!!".

At the North I enjoyed getting an enquiry and seeing it through from beginning to end, using your initiative. My confidence had returned.

I was nightshift when a man arrived at the office.   He had come back from Jersey because he wanted to confess to stealing a watch twelve years before.   He was a recovering alcoholic and now he had his life in order wanted to set the record straight.   Our reports did not even go that far back but he was most insistent, and so

I began by calling at the locus of the theft, the flat of his previous partner. The person was still there but did not want any action taken or to renew their previous relationship. Back at the office, the fellow seemed pleased but reluctant to leave. He then confessed that he had an early morning return ticket to Jersey, but was afraid of spending an evening in Glasgow alone in case temptation became too much and he succumbed to drink. I spoke with the Inspector on duty who agreed to bend the rules as it was quiet and allow Frank to spend the night in a cell, but the door would have to be closed. This raised another problem. Not only was Frank an alcoholic, he was also claustrophobic. I then telephoned the Social Work Department, but their night staff required a thousand forms in triplicate !!! I was fast running out of ideas when I remembered the Homeless Unit with whom I had built up a fairly good relationship. In desperation I explained our predicament. The place was full but Jimmy agreed, between ourselves, to put a mattress down on the floor and provide Frank with a breakfast before he caught his plane. Some time later, a postcard arrived at the office from Jersey thanking me. Another triumph for common sense over rules and regulations.

On nightshift, if an incident was deemed serious enough, then the Detective Chief Inspector had to be contacted and given the opportunity to attend. On one such occasion, John telephoned Norrie and advised him of the circumstances. As everything appeared under control, Norrie declined to come to the office, but later that night, something else occurred and John again telephoned. This time Norrie decided it merited his attention and John went out to his house to collect him. On the way back to the office, Norrie praised him "You were quite right to call me out son, it's a serious enquiry", but then added "that daft wee boy called me earlier on with a silly wee thing". John never admitted that he was also the "daft wee boy".

Blackhill was also part of "D" Division.   It was a war zone and the small police office had a notice on the wall which read "if you find the back door barricaded, expect an attack from the front".

One woman asked the indoor cop to sign her son's photograph for his application for a passport.   "The Soshul's taken him away furra hoaliday" she explained "It's goat tae be someone that knows im well that signs the photie an ah jist thoat ... well thurs naebody knows im better than you".

Another boy on the run for ages handed himself in because the school was going to Aviemore and he didn't want to miss that.

A young boy was ostensibly taking us to where he had disposed of stolen property, but at one point decided to play silly buggers and a struggle ensued.   His attempt to escape was over in seconds, but back at the office, I discovered my watch missing.   When our enquiries were completed and he was being released, I told him that he had three days to find my watch.   If he returned it to me in that time, I would not report his case to the Sheriff Court, I would send it to the lesser District Court (where it was going anyway).   The next day when I reported for duty I was told that a boy had handed in a watch apologising most profusely that the strap was broken.

One evening a householder reported that five young boys had called at her house with a collecting can purporting to be representing some charity. We found them in the street approaching passers-by and brought them to the office. Their parents were contacted to come and collect them and it was explained that the matter would be reported to the Children's Panel. Everyone hated juvenile cases. The amount of paperwork involved was horrendous and a total waste of time as nothing happened to them when they eventually appeared. I completed the case, but twice it came back from the boss asking some trivial questions. Eventually I put it in my drawer intending to get back to it when I had the time, but I promptly forgot about it. A few months later, I had cause to visit the mother of one of the boys on an unrelated matter. Quite sincerely she told me "well it cannae hiv been ma John cause ah tellt him he's no getting oot until that other thing comes up". I often wonder how long he was confined to the house.

As in every area, it was a small minority in Blackhill who were constantly to blame. There were some decent people, like the wee man who called at the office regularly to chat. One night he was really pleased because he had got himself a job filling in holes in the road .... "well", he confided importantly ..."you call them holes, we call them depreshuns".

Workers felt they had an impossible task in Blackhill when it was decided to build a community hall. Equipment was constantly stolen and the incomplete building vandalised. After completion it was broken into on numerous occasions.

This minority were also vicious thugs. On dealing with a serious assault in the area, witnesses were threatened and their houses came under siege on several occasions when bottles, bricks, and lumps of concrete were thrown through the door and windows.   The mother of one witness told me she had sent her son to relatives in Southern Ireland and he was not coming back.   She had been told that if he gave evidence, he would come home in a box.   I could not blame these witnesses and I felt very let down by the Sheriff when the witnesses who did appear to give evidence had to face concealed gestures and threatening facial expressions from the accused's relatives in the public benches, despite our pleas to the Sheriff to clear the Court.

All this prepared me for my next move .....

CHAPTER TWENTY SIX

EASTERHOUSE

In 1953, plans were approved to build Easterhouse, now one of Glasgow's four major housing schemes, at one time reputedly as big as Perth. The original inhabitants came mainly from the slum areas of Glasgow where there was overcrowding, outside toilets and no baths. Easterhouse offered a new start with its green fields, clean air and of course spacious rooms, inside toilets and baths, but there were problems from the outset. In their anxiety to build houses, the planners forgot completely about the social aspects. There were no shops or leisure facilities and children were bussed back into the city to attend school.

Initially the law was upheld from a caravan and it was not until 1973 that a permanent police office in Bogbain Road, Easterhouse replaced the temporary accommodation serving a population of about 80,000 people not only in Easterhouse, but also the areas of Swinton, Craigend, Riddrie, Garthamlock, Queenslie, Ruchazie and Cranhill.

If I thought "D" Divisional Headquarters was busy when I arrived there, I was totally unprepared for my arrival at Easterhouse in 1978. It was a sunny morning as I parked my car in the yard and made my way up the back stairs. Before I even pushed open the door leading into the C.I.D. office, I could hear the activity – raised voices, accusations, denials, files being thrown down on desks, feet moving hurriedly from one room to another.

As I stepped into the melee, I was greeted by several officers hurrying past me "hi, welcome to the madhouse". One figure paused for a second, "I'm Gordon, your neighbour, we've got an Easterhouse saga, you've got a custody case but I've dictated it for you. It's at the typists", and off he rushed. I could see four rooms, one for Detective Constables, one for Detective Sergeants, the Inspector's office and a waiting area, but all were full of people and property. I stood mesmerised clutching my polythene bag containing my worldly possessions as doors opened and closed around me. This chaotic scene occurred on a number of occasions when there was an Easterhouse saga.

Later when the night shift had managed to get off home to bed and some sort of sanity prevailed, I was faced with my first test. Initially my desk was in the Detective Sergeant's room, but I found the drawers full of paperwork. Two young acting Detective Constables (temporary C.I.D. officers) told me that they didn't have a desk and so they had decided to share what was supposed to be mine. I paused for a moment, realising that my next move was not going to be popular, but also realising that if I was going to survive as the sole woman in this tough environment, I would have to stand up for myself. I smiled and told them how sorry I was that now I had arrived they wouldn't have a desk anymore. Later the Inspector told me that he had been aware of the situation but decided to wait and see how I handled it. After a few months when the Constables room was re-designed I moved in there and one of the acting Detective Constables eventually became one of the best neighbours I ever had.

Easterhouse was a fascinating place to work, a place of extremes. It was said that every crime in the book was committed in our area, and yet I remember feeling rather ashamed when my own Minister announced from the pulpit that the people of Easterhouse contributed more in their Church collections than my own more affluent congregation, and one year the Easterhouse collection for Christian Aid was one of the highest in Scotland.

On the other side of the coin was the vicious, dishonest, territorial element. Gangs were prevalent such as The Drummy, Provy Rebels, Pak, Torran Toi, Baltoi and Cobbie Niggers. If a girl had a boyfriend who stayed outwith her area, he would walk her to the boundary and leave her there. It was safer for her to walk home herself. It would have been suicidal for him to enter her area. Battles between opposing gangs were common and the following is an actual example of injuries regularly recorded

Eleven stab wounds to the face, chest, abdomen and back.

Lacerations to left ear and eye, punctured left lung and severe bruising (all sustained by one victim)

An actual charge of serious assault read

Strike him on the head and body with bricks, bottles, pieces of concrete, a hammer and an axe, and stab him with a knife or similar instrument

The decent side of Easterhouse showed through on a number of occasions, none more so than when a uniform Sergeant was being severely beaten up by a gang of youths. A woman shouted down from her window to the arriving cavalry "you'd better get round the corner, your mate's getting a hammering". Without her, it would undoubtedly have been a lot worse as the incident was completely outwith the view of the officers.

That was Easterhouse.   You could visit one flat which was like a palace with photographs of offspring in graduation gowns adorning the mantelpiece and downstairs you would find a filthy hovel with the infamous tacky floors and distinctive but unidentifiable odour.   It was sad to hear of people who had not been out of their houses, as a couple, for years because of aggressive, anti-social, criminal neighbours who would take the opportunity to break into their houses if they realised the couple were out.   An early morning call to one of these hovels was not a good start to one's day, especially if it had to be searched.   There was one place always left to the end ….. the hall cupboard.   This was a narrow edifice into which enough clothes to stock a charity shop were crammed (dirty of course).   After searching it, the inevitable would happen.   An excruciating itch, the type which you cannot ignore, would develop, which necessitated an acrobatic movement with the back of your wrist or elbow in order to alleviate it.   If the ned was being removed to the office, he would casually extract a jumper and denims from the bottom of the pile.   Clean underpants was an optional extra seldom bothered about.   I came to the conclusion that they worked on the principal that the grime would be forced out by the weight of the other clothing on top.

Our clientele were not easily embarrassed.   On an early morning call a completely naked man answered our knock.   He invited us in and Willie gestured that perhaps he would like to cover himself up.   He apologised, cupped his hands over his private bits, about turned and quite unperturbed waddled down the long hall in front of us doing a "moonie" the whole way.

On the other hand, a cop was left very embarrassed one nightshift. He was checking the back of some shops on his beat and decided to relieve himself. Midstream, two neds jumped from the back window of one of the shops and took the time to shout some disparaging remarks before disappearing into the darkness. They were never apprehended.

Everyone in authority tried to play down the amount of crime committed in Easterhouse and I often remember answering the nightly telephone call from a reporter and informing him that everything was quiet as all hell raged around me.

There was a camaraderie at Easterhouse like nowhere else. I was one of the boys and it was us against the world. We likened ourselves to the Hill Street Blues television programme, and I was always sorry I didn't write to them for an autographed photograph which we could have displayed in our office. Those with ambition at Headquarters were almost frightened of us. Being sent to Easterhouse could seriously damage their career prospects. Visiting night shift Superintendents usually walked into the uniform bar, saw the mayhem and retreated quickly before they saw or could be involved in anything.

Occasionally some wonderful plan would be implemented, like the day the joiner arrived unannounced to fit locks to our bottom drawers. We were all issued with a key and instructed that the drawer was to be kept locked when not in use or on our days off. It didn't really make any difference, with a well developed Easterhouse mind, when you wanted something from another person's drawer, you just pulled out the drawer above.

One lunchtime we were having a saga when a uniform with braid appeared and announced to no-one in particular that he was from the P.R.U. Puzzled we all paused for a moment looking at each other before returning to growl at the subjects of our saga. "Is the C.I.D. clerk available?" he shouted hesitantly above the chaos. In unison we yelled "no, he's out". More growling. He continued valiantly "should I come back later?".

"Yes".

With that he disappeared back to Cowards Castle, and we never saw him again, although a Chief Constable's Directive did arrive at the office advising us that P.R.U. stood for the Procedures and Review Unit and was established in 1975 to ensure that all policies of the Chief Constable were being carried out ….. I think we failed.

Another decree emanating from Headquarters and undoubtedly of mind boggling importance was to the effect that only two box files were to be visible on the work top. This posed a problem for me. I was very methodical in my paperwork which necessitated three box files …. one for my crime reports, one for my cases, and one for "things" which did not fall into either category. Even the Inspector would on occasions ask me to deposit some particular piece of Headquarters bumph in my miscellaneous file. He tried on several occasions to coax me into relegating my miscellaneous file to my drawer but he failed miserably, and conceded when the Sheriff Court Production Department accused Gordon and I of failing to lodge a production. I was able to produce the all important receipt duly stamped by them from Box File 3 and they were forced to admit it was their mistake. He also learned to his horror that Sam's filing system consisted of a pile of empty cigarette packets in his bottom drawer each with some relevant information thereon. Suddenly my Box File 3 paled into insignificance.

In Headquarters at Pitt Street, there is a museum with interesting artefacts from various crimes. Our equivalent in Easterhouse was our collection of footwear on the flat roof adjacent to our room. It began with local hoodlums tossing up an odd shoe and we decided to add to it with contributions from various neds brought into the office. We were quite proud of our display of shoes, boots and trainers and even the neds considered it a status thing to have contributed an item. We were quite sad when it all had to be removed prior to an impending visit from some dignitary. We also had an odd assortment of junk which the Inspector instructed had to be disposed of. My goodie bag included a garden gnome with a large chip out of his red pointed hat, two screwdrivers and a copy of a Beatles tour programme. A woollen jumper and a sleeping bag went to an old man who had taken up residence in a tent like construction on a spare piece of ground in Springburn Road, who thought Christmas had arrived early.

Trying to get stationery was abysmal and we only got what nobody else wanted. I was very embarrassed when I attended a housebreaking at a school and while talking to the headmaster realised I was picking up the paper clips which were scattered around and was placing them carefully in my pocket. When I apologised and explained the reason for my actions, he obviously felt sorry for us and told me to help myself.   Back at the office there was great excitement as I shared out my spoils.

I realised one day just how differently you dealt with problems in Easterhouse compared to other areas.

Willie and I received information that cases of whisky had been stolen from a warehouse. A car had been seen acting suspiciously at the locus and two versions of the registered number were given.   In one version, the registered owner stayed in Easterhouse and in the other the owner stayed in the Lenzie area.

Our enquiries in Easterhouse went as follows ....

"Aye hullo, polis, we've had information that your car was spotted getting some stolen whisky loaded into it. We know it's probably rubbish.   Somebody wants to get at you for some reason.   You don't mind us having a wee quick look round, then if we get the same info. again we know it's rubbish".

Obviously this bit of chat is designed to hopefully eliminate the time consuming necessity of obtaining a warrant which it did on this occasion ..... BUT ..... on walking up the gravel driveway of the detached double garaged mansion, the above request for a wee quick look round did not seem appropriate.   Willie's solution for all these situations was "we'll play it by ear".   As the dying notes of some chiming orchestral piece echoed around the house, the door was opened by a well dressed businessman.   We identified ourselves "good evening, Strathclyde C.I.D."   The gentleman looked amazed and impressed "that was quick.   I've just reported it.   Have you got it back already?".   He continued that he had parked his car at the railway station and on his return when he finished work, it was gone.   We declined his invitation of a coffee and returned to Easterhouse.

Not long after my arrival in Easterhouse, I was "chatted up" by one of the uniform cops who tried to entice me out with promises of a meal at an expensive establishment. I declined which was the usual sensible tactic until I found out more about him.   I later learned that he had apparently dated the rather dubious mother of an even more dubious family.   It became quite a joke that I was his second choice after Mrs. C.   The story goes that one quiet nightshift, his car was spotted in a local car park with the lights out.   The panda cars contacted each other and quietly surrounded his vehicle.   At a given signal, they all switched on their lights and sounded their klaxons.   The tales of what happened next vary and have obviously been embellished through time, but suffice to say he was not at all amused.

Andy was a very enthusiastic officer, but always appeared with very long involved cases.   After being caught out on one occasion, a more experienced officer told me not to accept anything from him until he had sorted everything out and the offenders had been charged.

Because of his erratic manner, the following incident was not really taken seriously when he radioed in to say that a light aircraft which had just flown over his location, had only one landing wheel down.   The civilian radio controller passed the message to the Sergeant who decided foolish though it seemed, Glasgow Airport should be notified.   It transpired that the instruments on the plane were indicating that everything was in order, but when the control tower did a visual check, sure enough one of the two sets of wheels had not come down. The pilot was alerted and eventually managed to lower the wheel and land safely. Andy was an overnight hero, and the press wanted to interview him. Headquarters, anxious for the good publicity, thought it a great idea, but after a 'phone call from the hierarchy at Easterhouse decided against it.

CHAPTER TWENTY SEVEN

CHARACTERS AND MORE BESIDES

The uniform branch was full of characters with such nicknames as Dr. Death, Signal – the tube with the stripes, Harpic – clean round the bend, Tiger – a wild animal with stripes and the Olympic Torch – never goes out. Even the neds nicknames included Mad Patch and Pirate. Pirate was unique in that on one of the many occasions he was brought into the office, he confided that he had applied to join the police. He thought he would be an asset as it took a ned to spot a ned. We all thought he was kidding until someone thought they would check with the recruiting office ….. just in case. Sure enough he had applied. They were quickly told to dispose of his application form without further enquiry.

Some quite bizarre happenings occurred when our villains partook of their favourite pastime – glue sniffing or snue gliffing as it was called. The smell from them was horrendous, and any time spent with them gave you a headache and made you nauseas. One guy arrived at the office demanding to know who was responsible for the disgraceful condition of the small triangular piece of grass at the front of the office. He was incensed until given permission to organise the grass cutting himself. Off he went to obtain a lawn mower. Needless to say we never saw him again. The effects of the glue wore off and so did his civic pride.

The C.I.D. also had its characters. There was Sam and Eddie, known as the Beechgrove Gardeners, so called because as a hobby they bought young plants in bulk, nurtured them and sold them on to their colleagues. One quiet nightshift we found large sheets of polythene which we stuck from the ceiling to the floor around their adjacent desks.   To this erection, we placed a notice "The Beechgrove greenhouse".

Sam was a very easy going person who kept calm when all around were panicking.   He would spend ages chatting to neds, gleaning any little bits of information which he jotted down on his cigarette packet.   One guy did reveal to me that he would disclose all his secrets eventually just to get away from Sam's slow monotonous voice and long silences.

Sam was having great problems with his false teeth and out on a call one day asked the very decent occupants of the house if he could use their toilet to which they readily agreed.   A few minutes later he emerged with a wide grin "that's much better thanks" he smiled innocently as his embarrassed neighbour sat, realising like the couple, that the toilet had not been flushed.

His neighbour came back from Court one lunchtime and seriously told us not to mention Sam's pink hair.   As Sam walked in, we all sat engrossed in our sandwiches, until one brave guy could resist it no longer "Sam, your hair's pink".   Sam's face turned a deeper shade than his hair "bloody stupid woman.   I'll murder her when I get home.   Fancy putting her hair rinse beside the shampoo".   We all sympathised, but the general consensus of opinion was that it was a Sam's rinse gone wrong.

Dennis was the office Casanova.   He was nicknamed Zebedee because of an infamous time when he was talking on the 'phone and we all crept quietly up behind, in time to hear him whisper "I'm standing here like a coiled spring". We all burst out laughing shouting "b'doing! B'doing!"

On a late shift, Willie and I decided to treat ourselves to an Indian carry out as the previous night's delicacy, a hamburger from a stall, had given us both a mild attack of embarrassing food poisoning. In the dim romantic lights of the restaurant, which was outwith our area, we spotted Dennis sitting with a young lady. It was an opportunity too good to miss. When we returned to the office, I 'phoned the restaurant explaining that I knew a Mr Smith was dining there. I described him and explained that it was imperative I speak to him. I then hung up. The next day we listened stone faced as Dennis explained how the waiter had come up to the table and told him there was a lady on the 'phone for him. He was panic stricken for days wondering if it had been his wife or a private detective. I cannot print his comments when we eventually put him out of his misery.

Our boss thought it hilarious when one dashing officer instructed a witness that if she wished to contact him, his name was D.C. Prince …. as in Prince Charming. "Oh" replied the witness in all innocence "Ah wiz thinking mair a Prince the dug". However the Detective Inspector wasn't too happy a few days later when a witness whom he had interviewed and whose statement he had typed the previous day returned, asking to speak to the male typist.

The Easterhouse accent initially was difficult to understand and having returned from a fire in a school, I had noted St. Fenogs, St. Fenocks, St. Fenix, only to learn it was St. Thenogs.

I was not one for using the "F" word, but it was necessary on occasions for effect, and it became a source of amusement amongst my colleagues as to when I had worked myself up to the point when I could utter this oath.

A Constable also suffering from a language problem took a report of a stolen vehicle from a Chinese gentleman. As he reported the theft over his radio, he advised the controller that it was a 423 model. The Chinese gentleman interrupted "no no officer, a Ford Capri model".

Another officer was getting fed up with a ned giving a voluntary statement who was constantly giving nicknames and warned him to use proper names. In his next breath, the ned named "Freeby Boyce". The exasperated officer rasped "I've told you, no more nicknames". The ned looked puzzled "That's no a nickname". Sarcastically the officer replied "Freeby ... that can't be a first name". The ned looked relieved "naw, no Freeby Boyce .... Free wee boys (three wee boys).

It was nice to know that it wasn't just us who had difficulty however. A letter from a lawyer's office read "regarding the theft of a noddy motor car (an Audi motor car).

About this time, Headquarters came up with another wonderful idea, whereby neds were to write the preamble to a voluntary statement, which would add to its authenticity in Court. We were not allowed to assist them with the writing or with the spelling, but they forgot that many of our clientele could hardly read or write. I remember one statement read "I have been weaned by Deecee Scoot".

Gordon, my first neighbour, and I had a very good

working relationship, but he operated very much by the book and was horrified at some of the chances I took. In one case a man, who had never been in any kind of bother in his life, and his young son were travelling on the upper deck of a bus. He became annoyed at the foul language being used by a group of loud mouthed thugs and asked them to modify it. He was then subjected to more abusive language including threats. None of the other terrified passengers supported him and he became frightened, producing a pen knife. In the ensuing melee, one of the youths was stabbed. The police were summoned and the man was detained. His wife was contacted and collected their distraught son. As a weapon had been used, the C.I.D. became involved and I later received a 'phone call from his wife to say that the little boy who suffered from severe asthma, had just had a bad attack and she had called out the Dr. Apparently the lad was very close to his dad and was having panic attacks, aggravating his asthma. I instructed the mother to contact her Dr. and give him permission to confirm to me the boy's condition which he did. I then arranged for the father to be released on an undertaking that he would attend at the office first thing in the morning to be taken down to Court. He assured me that he would not let me down, which fortunately he didn't.

In another case, a gentleman called at the office on a Saturday afternoon with a complicated story regarding his motor vehicle. At the time it appeared to be a civil matter but when he returned a few days later with additional information, it was obvious that it merited police investigation. The case led me into the complex world of second hand car dealing where cars exchanged hands for cash, for another vehicle, or for a combination of both. The complainer had exchanged his Ford Cortina for a Ford Escort. The accused then re-possessed the Escort with a concocted story and supplied in its place a Llada, which he removed a few days later to effect an agreed repair, replacing it with a Volkswagen. The complainer was not satisfied with the condition of the Volkswagen which the accused then took away. The gentleman never saw any of the vehicles again, which we discovered had been re-sold. I eventually traced the new owner of the Llada motor car and had the unpleasant task, on the instructions of the Procurator Fiscal, of removing the vehicle to the police compound. I also called at the house of the new owner of the Ford Cortina and was informed by his mother that he was working. I asked that he call at Easterhouse Police Office which he did. When I explained the circumstances to the young nineteen year old, he was devastated. It was his first car for which he had saved very hard and had spent a lot of money on repairs and cosmetic surgery. When I told him that I was going to have to re-possess the car, he crumpled "please, you can't do that, it's outside. My girlfriend is sitting in it. It's her birthday. We're going for a run in it". He was a decent hardworking young man with no previous convictions. My next decision had Gordon reaching for his nerve pills. I suggested to the lad that the car wasn't outside the office, but he would bring it the next morning. Eventually he caught on to what I was saying and, thanking me profusely, left the office, as I emphasized that his failure to turn up would cost me my job. Gordon told me I was mad, but the next morning he was waiting for me as I took up duty. It really was a despicable crime. Hire Purchase Agreements complicated the issue and to my knowledge neither decent, law abiding citizen got their car back.

During this enquiry, Willie and I called on a reputable and well known car dealer. After our interview, Willie stopped to admire the most beautiful car I had ever seen at close range. I was gobsmacked when Willie told me it was a bargain at £5,000. "But it's new" I spluttered. Willie told me it was a demonstration model. My mind was already wondering how much I would get for my little white Volkswagen Beetle which had replaced the maroon A40 a few years previously and calculating how I could stretch my finances to buy this flashy red poser's dream. I then remembered that Willie had seen it first, but he assured me he wasn't interested. Seeing my excitement, he called over the assistant "how much did you say this was?" "The Audi Quatro ... £15,000 ... interested?" enquired the salesman. "A bit much for us" replied Willie with a twinkle in his eye. Everyone back at the office found out about my £5,000 dream machine.

A young man was luckier when five vehicles were broken into during the night and their radios stolen. We recovered his one which had been thrown over a hedge. Eventually we arrested the thieves who told us they couldn't sell the discarded one as it was a cheap model. He was delighted to get his radio back and we never told him how it had come about.

I was settling in very nicely at Easterhouse and enjoying the pay offs which occurred for whatever reason. I happened to mention to my colleagues a fact that every policewoman knew, but they didn't, that Cally Speshuls

(Carlesburg Special Brew) appeared to weaken a girl's resolve. They were quite intrigued. At the next pay off, I was greatly amused when they revealed that as I didn't like whisky, they had got me ... you've guessed ...a Cally Speshul. I explained that I didn't really like the stuff and in future a lager would do. That night I had a backhanded compliment paid to me when Dennis confided in all seriousness that I had a great figure. As I was about to modestly thank him, he added "if you had bigger boobs!!".

At another pay off, when one of the boys was leaving due to promotion, he produced the statutory bottle of whisky. As the day shift relaxed in the back room, the late shift brought in a well known housebreaker. Feeling in a benevolent mood and knowing he would not see the ned again, Eric offered him a glass of whisky. The ned's eyes lit up and his hand shot out greedily but at the last minute he paused and sniggered "hah, you don't get me as easy as that. You just want ma prints on the glass. Think ahm stupit". We all took turns of trying to convince him that it wasn't a set up, but he would have none of it.

The clientele at Easterhouse always liked to think that they were one step ahead of you. On a late shift, a man approached us in the street. He was acting in a very secretive manner, constantly looking over his shoulder and whispered that he had information for us. This was quite unusual but we encouraged him to continue. Finally he confided that he knew where the missing racehorse Shergar was but he needed some money in advance before he could reveal the exact location. We declined the offer, but who knows, maybe Shergar was

living in the lap of luxury three up in a close in Easterhouse and we missed the golden opportunity of becoming famous.

Another young girl kept us all amused when she told
us that her father didn't work .... he goat the Infidelity
Benefit.

When one woman was being charged with the theft of
a purse containing two £5 notes and five £1 notes, she
was incensed "that's a bloody lie. Ther wiz only £6 in
ur purse".

Yet another woman reported that she had either lost
her purse or it had been stolen.   From our office she
went straight to the Church and lit a candle.   She was
delighted and became even more religious when on her
return home she got a 'phone call from us to say that her
purse and the £30 it contained had been handed in.

While at Easterhouse I had two complaints against
me.   In one, the ned accused me of chasing him around
the tables in the office.   It was completely untrue and I
was able to show the Complaints Department when they
arrived to investigate the matter that all the work tops
were affixed to the walls.

In the second, I was accused by the ned of stripping
him.   I had in fact asked him to remove his jacket and
roll up the sleeves of his shirt.   I also asked him to take
off his socks and shoes.   As I explained to the discipline
officer, having seen the colour and smelt his feet, there
is no way I would have asked him to strip.   I had asked
him the aforementioned because at a housebreaking
we were investigating, the perpetrator had left some
blood, having cut himself on the broken glass from the
window.

CHAPTER TWENTY EIGHT

SAD CASES

There was one ned who probably did have a genuine complaint against me.   A young girl confided in her mother that her brother was "mucking" about with her. The mother informed the social worker whose words I quote "he is only parroting his father.   He will grow out of it.   In the meantime keep an eye on him".   The background was that the father some years before had been convicted of interfering with the girl's two elder sisters who had since left the family home.   The incidents continued albeit spasmodically and the mother then approached the family Dr. who prescribed pills to be given to the teenager when the mother felt he needed them.   The mother of low intelligence felt that she had done all she could by approaching those in authority. Time went on and the young girl left school.   Having been a loner at school, she then went on to a Youth Training Scheme where she was befriended by another girl, who, on one occasion spent the night with the victim.   In the middle of the night, the brother attempted to climb into bed between them, but was chased from the room by the visitor to whom the young girl confided.   The visiting teenager repeated the story to her mum who immediately advised the victim's mother to contact the police. By this stage, this poor pathetic youngster was completely withdrawn and rocked backwards and forwards constantly, staring at the ground as I tried to gently coax the story from her.   Eventually from her pocket, she produced a crumpled piece of paper, the reply to a letter she had written to another brother, in jail for armed robbery. In it, he told her to tell her brother that if he didn't stop what he was doing, he would murder him on his release from prison. This was the only piece of security she felt she had to cling to.   When we went to arrest this individual, I was not really prepared for his total lack of remorse for the way he had used and abused his sister.   He simply shrugged his shoulders as I tried to get some re-action from him. I remember as we entered the Detective Sergeant's room, the Inspector was sitting quietly reading the newspaper enjoying his lunch.   The ned chose that moment to make a derogatory sneering comment about his sister. I seized him by his collar and pushed him on to a chair which toppled, landing him on the floor.   I don't know who got the biggest shock …me, him or …the Inspector who carefully picked up his sandwiches and coffee, tucked the newspaper under his arm and humming softly left the room closing the door behind him.   This horrible, filthy individual had every intention of pleading not guilty, thereby forcing his young victim to stand and tell a courtroom full of strangers the disgusting things she had to endure over a period of years.   I am not ashamed to admit that I reminded him of the contents of his brother's letter.   I am glad to say he had a change of heart and pled guilty. I often wonder what became of that poor girl.

Incest is a despicable crime due to the fact that the perpetrator is someone on whom the victim should be able to rely on and trust.

On a fine summer's day a few neighbours of one close were sitting chatting in the back court.   A thirteen year old girl went up to her house to use the toilet. When she didn't re-appear, her mum went looking for her. She found the door locked from the inside and looked through the letter box intending to call her daughter. What she saw was her semi-naked daughter on the bed with her father lying on top of her, obviously engaging in a sexual act. The woman became hysterical, shouting for someone to 'phone the police which they did. Again it was so difficult to gently prise the truth from this teenager who through reasons of loyalty, threats, confusion and guilt was reluctant to betray her father. Eventually she revealed that it had been going on for some time. I must confess I was disgusted when he received a sentence of only eighteen months, but very touched when the mother appeared at the office with a bunch of flowers to thank me for my kindness to them. I was therefore horrified some days later when the same lady trying to come to terms with what had happened, arrived in the office absolutely distraught. She had received a 'phone call from the prison psychiatrist asking if she would be taking her husband back on his release from prison and suggesting that in his, the psychiatrist's opinion, it had been partly her fault that it had happened because she did not give her husband "his way" when he wanted it (a fact she vehemently denied). This poor woman was being made to feel that she was partly at fault for what had happened to her daughter. We talked it over and the last I heard both mother and daughter were coping well without the father.

Every case in Easterhouse was different. Patsy was an overweight, tough, foul mouthed, volatile young woman who had come to the notice of the police on a number of occasions.   She had to be treated with caution and one day when she refused point blank to sit in the back seat of the C.I.D. car because "you never knew what these men would get up to", we diffused the situation by agreeing that I would sit with her.   We didn't pay much attention to this behaviour putting it down to another example of her awkwardness, until one night when we were called to her house by neighbours.   There we found Patsy with several severe slash wounds between her thighs.   It transpired that her father had been abusing her for years.   He found out that she had recently got herself a boyfriend and in a fit of jealous rage had assaulted her.

Some cases were extremely difficult and none more so than two girls brought to the office by their parents, suspected of being sexually molested by an older boy. Both girls were mentally retarded and attended a special needs school.   I interviewed Jean first and she told me they had their dinner the previous night at her auntie's and had then walked over to the park where they had met the accused and the alleged incident had taken place.   Jean and her mum then sat in the waiting room and I interviewed Helen along with her mum.   Helen corroborated that they had dinner at the auntie's, but then continued that they bought sweets and cans of juice and went to the back courts where they met the accused and a second version of the alleged incident took place.   Neither girl would alter her story and so I sat them opposite each other and said "so you both went over to the park after dinner".   Jean immediately piped up "aye we did". Helen re-acted "naw we didnae".   Staring each other in the eye, Jean replied "aye we did".   Back came the reply "naw we didnae". I counted ten "aye we did's", before I stopped them. Both parents agreed that it was pretty hopeless. They left the office quite satisfied that they would watch the girls more closely and took them to their own Dr. who confirmed that there were no signs of obvious interference.

Children were for obvious reasons very difficult to deal with. The Detective Sergeant on one occasion thought he was being helpful. I was taking a statement from a very tearful young newspaper boy who had been assaulted and had his paper money stolen. As Eric came into the office he nudged the poor lad and eyebrows drawn, gruffly advised him "now you tell this officer the truth or you'll have me to answer to". Quickly I pointed out to Eric that this was the complainer. Even quicker he responded "there you are now, that's what's going to happen to these boys when we catch them, so you just dry your tears".

A Detective Sergeant and myself were having an exhausting time with one boy, suspected of setting fire to his school. We really were on the point of giving up thinking that perhaps our information had been wrong, when my neighbour lit his pipe. We suddenly became aware of the effect that the flame was having. When Andy slowly moved the match from side to side, the boy followed it mesmerised. His eyes glinted and he became almost excited by it. We continued the questioning, now convinced that he was not so much a vandal but a boy with a real problem. He eventually confessed to lighting the fire, and Andy included our thoughts in the report to the Children's Panel.

A school teacher had the harrowing experience of

receiving indecent letters.   She suspected a few girls at the school, but had no proof and talking to them had not stopped the letters.   She eventually reported the matter to us.   I instructed her not to touch the letters and forwarded them to the Fingerprint Department where we got lucky and got one fingerprint.   I then asked all the girls accompanied by their parents to call at the office, where I explained the situation.   I asked for the co-operation of the parents in allowing me to take fingerprints from their offspring, and assured them that it was as much a case of clearing any suspicion hanging over their daughters as of finding the culprit.   One by one the girls allowed me to take their prints, but two were very hesitant, one even to the extent of attempting to smudge the imprint.   All the fingerprints were submitted to the Fingerprint Department who as suspected came up with the girl who had been most reluctant.   When they came into the office, the very decent parents were shocked and angry with their daughter who by this time, having had a few days to dwell on her silly actions, was in tears and only too willing to name her accomplice.

Although we had integration in the police, I could understand that it was far more preferable for a female officer to deal with some crimes.   However, in the cases of baby assaults which were extremely time consuming, I couldn't understand why they came automatically to me to deal with.   Most of my colleagues were fathers, whereas I had no children.   One morning, unaware that the Inspector had arrived and was in his office, I was complaining bitterly to my colleagues and telling them of my intention to speak to the Inspector.   When Gordon noticed that he was sitting in his room and had obviously heard me, I thought I might as well take the bull by the horns.

"Can I have a word with you Sir?"

"Of course".

O.K. so far I thought and continued like a lamb to the slaughter.

"All these baby assaults, do I have to do them?"

He looked at me for a second "yes".

I knew by his tone that there was no point in proceeding.

"Right" and I left his office.

I did notice, however, a few days later that a case was allocated to a male officer with a rider that he liaise with me.

I felt very sorry for one young girl who appeared at the office confessing to slapping her baby.   I had the baby examined by the police Dr. who ascertained that he was a well fed baby with no signs of old or recent injuries.   It transpired that she had recently moved into the area, a single mother without any contact with her parents and had not had time to cultivate any friends.   The baby cried constantly, but numerous visits to her Dr. revealed nothing wrong and he was just a "whingy baby".   She couldn't sleep and was utterly exhausted and perplexed. Probably now she would have been diagnosed as having post natal depression.   When the incident occurred, she panicked and came round to the office.   I understood her feelings.   I felt my own nerves on edge as the baby never stopped crying the whole time he was in the office. A quick 'phone call to the Social Works Department did more good than any court case.

Although on many occasions I did not see eye to eye

with the Social Works Department, I have to admit that, like us, they have a very difficult job which is surrounded in red tape.

The mother in this case was single, looking after two children six years and five months. They came to our attention when a neighbour reported that the mother had been drunk the previous day and the children had been howling. When the uniform cops called, she was sober, very co-operative and the children appeared well fed and contented. A few weeks later the same neighbour had to help the family get into their house as they had locked themselves out. She noticed that the baby was soaking and on further discreet examination, his bottom was red raw. She then reported the matter to the Social Services who called at the house, but again nothing seemed untoward. More time elapsed until the police were called again. This time men were discovered in the house. The children were screaming and the mother was drunk. The children were removed and the drunken mother was arrested for kicking her neighbour's door, blaming her for contacting the police. She was eventually released when sober and the children returned to her, but the Social Services began calling on a regular basis. The neighbour reported to them that the six year old was begging for food and she regularly heated up soup for the baby, who on one occasion she brought in from his veranda where he was lying partially naked as snow fell around. When one of the children ended up in hospital with pneumonia, the Social Services warned the mother but still continued to try and keep the family together and organised through a voluntary organisation for the house to be redecorated.

On occasions the older boy was found to have scratches and bruises which he always explained were due to him falling.   The school gave him shoes as he wore plastic sandals in all weathers, but they would disappear after a few days, when he would say he lost them.   It was a very difficult case as the children didn't appear undernourished.   A Dr. who examined the older boy only confirmed that his few minor injuries were consistent with a fall, and it was a recorded fact that the two neighbours for whatever reason didn't get on.   On this occasion, the Social Services decided that their only course of action was to keep a close watch on the family.

On the next occasion, however, we <u>ALL</u> failed a little girl terribly, although even on hindsight I cannot see with all the regulations and laws, what else we could have done.   She was four years old when I received the file for enquiry from the Social Works Dept, who had reluctantly reported it to us as they could not gain access to the house to investigate reports of bruising and a burn mark resembling contact with a steam iron on the little girl's arm.   She stayed with her mother and stepfather but also spent a lot of time with her grandparents.   I remember the Saturday well.   I spent the whole afternoon with the mother, stepfather and little girl.   She refused to let me see her arm even with bribes of sweets or sounding the "mee maw" (klaxon) in the police car, and protested and wriggled constantly to get off her mum's knee.   All afternoon she repeated one phrase in answer to my questions "I fell over".   Her mother explained that she had a blind spot in her eye and didn't see some obstacles causing her to fall quite often.   By the end of the afternoon, I had achieved nothing.   I began to seriously consider the grandparents as she spent a lot of time with them, and arranged for them to call at the office on the Sunday. As I watched the family leaving, I had no way of knowing then that I would never see the little girl again.   On a bright Sunday morning the grandfather arrived telling me that his wife was too upset to come to the office. For a second, my doubts were raised, but then he told me that his granddaughter had died during the night at the Royal Infirmary. I immediately contacted my Detective Inspector who took over the enquiry, arranging for a police post mortem to be carried out. It was the worst moment of my career, when I was asked by my Inspector to formally identify the body prior to the post mortem as this could not be done by the parents or grandparents who were all in effect, suspects.   It was a horrible task to look down on the innocent, naked little girl who the previous day had sat in the office so fiercely defending the person who had inflicted her injuries, and now lying stretched out on that cold, impersonal, white porcelain slab.   I did my duty and asked the Inspector if it was necessary for me to remain during the post mortem.   It wasn't and as I quickly left that horrible scene, I can still hear the high pitched whine as electric saw grinded into bone.   It was established that she died from peritonitis caused by punching or kicking to her abdomen.   Later her 6'4" stepfather confessed to inflicting the injury. Even her grandparents when interviewed stated they had noticed bruises on her frequent visits to them and had questioned her, but such was her misplaced loyalty, fear, or for whatever reason, even at that tender age, she told them that she had fallen.   I think in all our minds …. Mother, grandparents, Social Works Dept. and in mine was ….. "if only".

To emphasize the difficulties in such cases, a father, mother and adopted teenage daughter arrived at the office, all in a distressed state. The daughter had been constantly running away from home and had eventually confided in her mother that her father had been interfering with her.   When the mother confronted the poor man, he was the one who insisted they come to the police office.   Exhaustive enquiries were made relating to times and dates the incidents were meant to have occurred etc., and finally a medical examination which could find no evidence relating to the extent of the abuse alleged by the girl.   She later confessed that she did not think things would have got so out of hand and had concocted the story as a way of getting back at her father who had been chastising her for her various misdemeanours and laying down some house rules.   She was eventually placed in a home due to her unruly behaviour and assaulted one of the nuns.

Another very sad case occurred about 10.00 pm one night when a man called at the uniform bar to report that his ten year old daughter had been missing for an hour.   A few details were taken and he was told to make a thorough search of his house and to check with all her friends, relatives etc.   Meantime the uniform officers on the street were alerted to keep a look out for her.   At midnight the father returned along with a nineteen year old neighbour who said that about 8.20 pm he had asked the girl to get him some ciggies and ginger from the ice cream van which she had done.   This appeared to be the last sighting of her.   A recognised procedure then swung into action and a Sgt. returned to the house of the neighbour. He explained to him that as he was the last person to have seen her, his house would have to be searched. The young man was only too willing to help. In a bedroom, the Sgt. came across a locked wardrobe. The man explained that there was nothing in it, the key having been lost for some time. The Sgt. apologised but said that he would have to break it open to which the man replied that he quite understood. The wardrobe door was forced and it was found to be empty except for a large black polythene bin bag. The man stood silently as the Sgt. pulled the heavy bag from the wardrobe and opened it up. In it, he found the young girl's limp body, her clothes wrapped around her head.

My neighbour and I attended the call initially until the Detective Inspector and Chief Inspector arrived, and my recollection is of a man sitting quietly composed showing little emotion even when in the middle of the melee of uniformed officers, C.I.D. officers, police photographers, and Scenes of Crime officers, his wife arrived home. She had been visiting her parents to show off their newly born baby. She was as devastated as the parents of the poor little girl.

CHAPTER TWENTY NINE

AND MORE

I have to say that in Easterhouse we had very few genuine cases of rape. About 5.00 am nearing the end of a busy nightshift, a drunk elderly woman was helped in, complaining bitterly of being raped. As we listened patiently to her various rambling versions of the event, she spent some considerable time separating a small amount of tobacco into three and spreading each portion thinly along a cigarette paper. She interrupted her story long enough for a furred up, discoloured old tongue to protrude from her mouth and expertly run along the full length of the thin paper. Continuing the saga, she slowly rolled her creations carefully between dirt ingrained fingers and broken nails, until sealed. Finally she concluded, sat back and declared "and that's what happened". She then lit a cigarette, inhaled deeply, examined the thin paper wedge between her fingers, nodded with satisfaction and offered one creation to me and the other to Willie. As neither of us smoked, we could honestly decline and she carefully and lovingly placed them in her coat pocket for after. "Oh and they stole ma brand new shoes". We decided to tour around with her to try and pinpoint the location of the alleged incident, and after a visit to several back courts, Willie found a pair of boots in fairly good condition. Initially she dismissed them but on closer inspection, she declared it was boots she had on not her new shoes. Back at the office over a cup of tea, she surveyed herself in the mirror in her newly acquired boots and decided the polis had enough to do and she did not want to be examined by a police Dr. or to take up any more of our valuable time.   She left the office a <u>very</u> satisfied customer.

The conditions in which some people live are totally unimaginable to the majority of us.   While on a call to a very well appointed flat, the lady mentioned that she was concerned about the smell coming from the house below her, the home of an elderly alcoholic who lived alone.   Feeling rather apprehensive, when we received no reply to our knocking, we found the door opened to our touch.   The smell in the dingy hall was appalling as we slowly walked along, calling as we went and pushing open creaking doors to reveal bare unfurnished rooms. At the end of the hall we entered the final room strewn with empty bottles.   In the dim light, a dirty, unshaven, elderly man lay drunk on a single bed amid filthy covers. A large old fashioned cooking pot was visible under the bed which we discovered was to hopefully catch anything seeping through the mattress caused by his incontinence.   As he had committed no crime and was not in need of hospital treatment, another call was made to the Social Works Department.

Drink played a big part in the behaviour of our clientele.   During a survey, it was found out that one of the pubs in Easterhouse took in more money than any other pub in Scotland.

One man decided while drunk that life wasn't worth living and left a note for his wife in which he told her to buy a drink for all his pals and concluded by telling her that heaven was a wonderful place and he loved her.   He then had more drink to wash down the pills, but with typical Easterhouse luck, he woke up in the Royal Infirmary and spent the next hour desperately trying to get in touch with his wife before she spent his money on a drink for his pals.

In the early hours of the morning, we called at the house of a very distraught mother whose teenage son had not returned home. As she explained that he never stayed out late unless he was going camping, father awoke from his drunken slumber on the couch and demanded to know what we were doing in his house and who told us we could come in. Mother interrupted "It's Joseph, he's no come home and you know he's always in by 10.30 pm"

"That's right enough", slurred father "unless of course he's gaun campin .....oh here ah furgoat tae tell ye ....he's away campin".
We hastily retreated as verbal abuse poured down on the hapless man.

It always amazes me the number of people who think that police cars are well maintained and in perfect running order. Not so, particularly in Easterhouse, where our C.I.D. cars ran on a wing and a prayer. It was a winter's night when the call came in to attend a murder. Our little 1100 motor car refused to start and our uniformed colleagues pushed us down the slight slope where it coughed feebly and came to life reluctantly. We spluttered all the way to the incident and read with some amusement the next day in the press "Murder squad detectives raced to the scene".

Murders were quite often the result of domestic abuse over years of Friday and Saturday drink binges.

In this tragic case, the woman had as usual prepared the meal, but on her drunken husband's return home, he had thrown it at her. As the plate smashed close to her head and its contents slowly slid down the wall, the years of abuse like lava from a smouldering volcano erupted and her hand closed around the handle of a kitchen knife by her side. With one blow the brute was dead.

When we arrived, she was sitting in a neighbour's house, and although murder can never be condoned, I felt nothing but pity for the pathetic, bewildered figure sitting in front of me. I wrote the following poem about her.

Whispering neighbours, what do they care
About the pathetic figure slouched in the chair,
Hair, dangling like pieces of string, head bowed,
The thin ashen face and the body cowed,
Uncontrollable shaking of bloodstained hands
Twisting a dirty handkerchief into countless strands.
Like the pendulum of a clock, she rocks to and fro,
As whispering neighbours come and go.
He, lies still on the kitchen floor,
His blood spattered over the walls and the door,
Congealing around the handle of the knife
Embedded in his chest, no sign of life.
No more drunken beatings, she had suffered enough,
Her bruised battered body, he thought he was tough.
Will time heal her memories, her faith in mankind.
Will the pain ever go that's going on in her mind.
She raises her head and stares into my eyes,
Is he ?, I nod, she shivers and sighs.
The tears, like rivers, roll down her face.
In court, she'll just be another case.

And the whispering neighbours, what do they care,
About the pathetic figure slouched in the chair.

In contrast, the following is an actual statement taken from a witness and demonstrates how easily matters get out of hand, bearing in mind that although humorous, it too could have resulted in a death.

"We were watching T.V. in the living room.   We heard ma ma telling ma auntie that the wallpaper she wiz pittin up ... she wisnae daen it right.   They started fightin an ma brother split them up.   Rab kept ma auntie in the living room and John pit ma ma in the kitchen and held the door closed.   Next thing the window smashed.   We looked oot, an ma ma wiz lying ootside oan the grun. Ma auntie ran doon the hall outside an they sterted shoutin.   Then ma auntie came in an she hud blood oan ur.   Rab brought ma ma intae the livin room an she wiz bleedin.   She'd been stabbed.   We goat an ambulance tae the Roayal".

In conclusion, ma would not stay in the hospital and signed herself out and would not press charges against auntie.

I always found it helpful in a situation where the husband was drunk if I could gain the co-operation of the wife.   I would turn my back on the husband knowing my neighbour was watching him and sympathise with the woman telling her in that confidential manner that only women have mastered, that I had one just the same at home, always giving me a showing up.   I didn't but nine times out of ten she would pull a face, raise her eyes to heaven, shake her head and ask what it was I wanted. Quietly I would get the information and we were out of the house while the husband was still objecting to our presence.

I asked one mother how her son was getting on, as we

hadn't seen him in the office for quite a while.   Proudly she told us "oh he hud a joab sweeping the streets". "Well good for him" I replied with genuine admiration. "Aye but he loast it".   "Aw" I commiserated.   "Aye, he wiz daen that well, but he cannae read, so he couldnae read the street names and kept sweeping the same streets twice".   I couldn't really think of an appropriate answer to that.   However she continued that now he was going to classes to learn to read, and so I wished him well.

Some mothers went to any lengths to defend their off-spring and we were faced with replies such as "He's no a bad boay.   He disnae break intae hooses, jist assaults and things" and the favourite "It couldnae be him.   He's jist oot the hoose".   But one mother was honest and realistic when asked what her son was going to do with his life.   "Ave nae idea, but it'll no be anything legal by the way".

When we got a new Detective Inspector, I found my lack of confidence returning when every night I found a distinctive piece of yellow paper from him questioning my actions from the previous night.   However the Detective Sergeant spotted my glum face reading yet another note and told me not to take it personally, everybody got them on nightshift.   "You just put them in the bucket, and he's so busy concocting new ones, he's forgotten the last ones" he advised me.   It worked, although then I began to feel a bit annoyed.   We were working through situations as they unfolded in the middle of the night, while he was perusing it sitting at his desk over a cup of coffee after a good night's sleep.

On one occasion, however, I could see that I was at fault. It was a clear night with a full moon. A dangerous time to be in Easterhouse. The word lunatic is derived from Lunar, and our nutters were certainly living up to it.

A serious stabbing had occurred in a house in a very bad street. Such was the atmosphere that night, that, in order to attend the call, we had a uniform car guarding our C.I.D. car and an officer at the window of the house watching them. The street lights had been smashed and the local loonies were making Indian wolf calls to each other across balconies and from back closes. The injured man's account of the incident read "I heard shouts and a smash at the door so I barricaded it. Then the living room window went in and a lump of concrete and a couple of posts came through the back window. The 'phone wires had been cut. They were using axes on the door and when they got in, they trashed the house. They were wearing crash helmets and masks".

When the ambulance arrived, the man insisted on walking out to it, the knife sticking out of his back and his hands held high above his head giving the "V" sign. Even the children that night were running around with camouflage paint on their faces.

In another street, we were confronted by a barricade of bins and rubbish. As we stopped the car, a gang came running down a path to the side of us whooping and carrying bin lids and pick axe handles. Willie did not often swear, but as he struggled with the gears I remember him shouting "Christ, where the fuck's reverse". We shot backwards chased by the mob, but as we passed a side street, a support unit vehicle with about five or six uniformed officers looking for action reached the junction in time to see a little 1100 motor car shooting past them in reverse.   With the arrival of the cavalry, the odds changed, and as the cops charged, the neds quickly went into retreat.   I guarded the cars and identified the neds as the hunters returned with their prey.   Quite a few prisoners were taken that night.

In all, we dealt with about four serious assaults and kept apologising profusely to the poor "on call" Dr. at the Royal Infirmary who had been working all day, was having no sleep on this crazy night, and would face another day shift.   It had just begun to quieten down, and we were arranging the statements, productions, annual leave sheets, and all the other bumph which makes up a case, into semi orderly piles on the work top in the main office, making sure that as much as possible had been done for the early shift C.I.D. officers coming on duty and being allocated the case, most of which that night was headed "This is an Easterhouse saga", when .... we were told to attend a local pub.   A man who had earlier on been ejected by staff after causing a disturbance, burst into the premises, went into the toilet and blasted a hole in the ceiling with a shotgun.   After some enquiries, we established who he was and did a search of his usual haunts.   The uniform branch were informed to keep a look out for him and we left that morning exhausted but happy that we had covered everything satisfactorily.   After all the previous events that night, quite honestly, this incident paled into insignificance as no-one had been injured.   On hindsight, one can realise the seriousness of an angry man walking around with a shotgun, but we had covered all avenues apart from informing the Detective Inspector who had apoplexy when he began working his way through the mountain of paperwork, over coffee of course, and found himself staring at the word "SHOTGUN". I have previously mentioned how delighted I was at being treated as one of the boys and I certainly was that day. As our clientele would say "he went mental by the way".

I discovered that equality had not reached Barlinnie Prison when we went there to charge a prisoner. It was my case, but I found the governor continually addressed my male colleague to the point of almost turning his back on me. When I told him I was ready to see the prisoner, he looked aghast "well, if you could just stay here and I'll take your partner along". I drew myself up to my full 5'5" and a half and gave him one of my "I'm in charge looks", informing him that both of us would be present. I would charge the prisoner and Willie would corroborate. He then revealed that this prisoner had a habit of stripping off in company. After assuring him that the sight of a naked man would not scar me for life, we were led from his domain to a waiting room where our potential Full Monty sat meekly at a desk. I immediately told him that I wasn't there to argue whether he was guilty or not guilty, I was only there to charge him. He listened patiently and then replied "aye fer enuff hen, ye cannae be ferrer than that". Crisis over.

It was quite common if a policewoman made an error of judgement for the comment to be made "well what do you expect from a polywumman". I therefore took great pleasure in reminding any cop who was silly enough to make this remark, of the poly man who recovered a stolen vehicle and was present when the owner arrived to retrieve it.   The owner pointed out that the large metal box on the back seat did not belong to him and so the two of them manhandled it into a nearby field.   The satisfied owner drove off and the cop made his way to the office for his refreshment break, only to learn that an office in the city centre had been broken into and their safe had been stolen.   One very embarrassed cop had to confess to his actions …. Ooops!

Gordon, my neighbour, was always determined to be a matchmaker and on nightshifts would constantly ask me "what about him?"

"Too young"

"Him?"

"Too old"

Occasionally I would say "he's quite nice".

Like a protective father figure he would retort "what, no way, he's a rat bag.   What about him?   He's a nice guy".

"Nope".

Finally to shut him up one night I told him that I quite liked Sgt. Scott but was sure he was married.   A few nights later, Gordon appeared with a smug look on his face "he's not married".

"Who's not married?"

"Sgt. Scott".

A short time later, while at a pay off at Baird Street, and much to the surprise of the colleague who had driven me there, Sgt. Scott approached me.   The fact that the ensuing relationship remained relatively secret and did not become common knowledge is entirely due to the few cops who spotted us together but said nothing.   On 2nd June 1980 we were married and I became Detective

Constable Scott much to the confusion of all my previous colleagues.

CHAPTER THIRTY

FIREARMS

I had still been qualifying as an authorised firearms officer and it had been decided that a week's course would be held. Much of it was outdoors where several scenarios were re-enacted, making it completely different from our straight forward indoor training.

One officer, and myself were instructed to approach, without being spotted, a man standing at the entrance to a building brandishing a firearm. Our progress was being monitored through binoculars by the training officers. We were advancing nicely crawling through the undergrowth, when my partner whispered "I've lost my gun". Our guns had been holstered but he had forgotten to fasten the safety strap. Still on our stomachs, we managed to crawl back retracing our steps until we found it. I swore to him that I would tell no-one, but later, on being questioned by the training officer as to our unusual tactics, he confessed, which our instructor then used as a lesson to us all.

Everyone had embarrassing moments. I led a search into an old empty barn like building containing a car. Slowly we progressed clearing the way as we went. When we reached the car we thoroughly searched it, eventually declaring the building safe, only to have our gunman leap from the wide ledge of a window half way along the building, which had been covered over by a piece of wood. Another lesson learned.

In another exercise, we had to progress through a

heavily wooded area, supposedly searching for escaped prisoners. It certainly made us realise the difficulties as we were constantly compromised by our instructors appearing behind us from hiding places in the undergrowth.

We also had to experience the effect of C.S. gas by going into a room filled with the acrid smoke. Although the instructor was suitably attired and had breathing apparatus, we had no such niceties. We had to write our names on a piece of paper on a desk. When I wrote Scott and headed for the door, he stopped me "you weren't always Scott were you?. I think you should write your maiden name". I was well and truly exposed to the gas by the time I burst out into the fresh air where I found the other victims. Wiping your eyes and nose made it worse and everyone carried out the advice to bend over and allow the fluid to stream from your stinging eyes and nose. A horrible sensation and experience which certainly gave an insight into the effects of the gas.

On our final day, we had to run twice around a field before firing at a target. Although I was exhausted, and my heart was pounding, I shot my highest ever score. I carried a gun on a few occasions, but fortunately never had to use it.

CHAPTER THIRTY ONE

BACK TO EASTERHOUSE

Although vicious weapons were used by the Easter-house neds, it was a rarity for guns to be used. However one day Kenny and Jim had committed some work misdemeanour and had been down at Divisional Headquarters to have their fingers rapped. On their way back to our office, they were commiserating with each other and one made the fatal mistake of deciding that they needed a good arrest to get themselves back in the good books. Almost on cue the radio crackled "Armed hold up in progress at the post office in Smithycroft Road". They were seconds away and acknowledged the call. They were in time to see two men exit the post office and on seeing Kenny and Jim they took off on foot. As they were being chased one actually shot at Jim, but both officers were successful in apprehending the two well known, vicious and dangerous criminals. Later, as they were congratulated by the very boss who earlier had given them the rollicking, Jim commented "I know we wanted something good, but not that good".

Much more common was the carrying of a "steakie". Returning to the office after our morning calls, Eric spotted a youth whom he knew was wanted on warrant. He was bundled into the back of the car. At the office, he was searched and a large penknife found "hah offensive weapon" smiled Eric. "That's nothing" sneered the ned "wait 'til you see the other one". When his jacket was opened, he had a large wooden handled knife (steakie) down the belt of his trousers with the point facing upwards.   He felt in this position, it was quicker to draw it out to chib someone.   However, although he didn't realise it, we realised how lucky he had been. When we pushed down his head to shove him into the car the point of the knife could have easily penetrated his body.

It was always nice to get a good result when a lot of work went into an enquiry. A vicious robbery had taken place from an ice cream van.   The neds had pulled the terrified occupants from the van and attacked them with pick axe handles.   I found hairs adhering to a black woollen hat discarded at the locus and identified by the witnesses as being worn by one of the accused.   When we later arrested suspects, hair samples were taken from all three and submitted to the laboratory who confirmed a positive match.   They later all pled guilty.

During that enquiry, a female detective Sergeant who had recently arrived at the office overheard us talking about the case.   With usual warped Easterhouse humour, I casually mentioned that the neds hadn't wanted to wait for the police doctor and so I had taken the head and pubic hair samples.   Her mouth opened, closed and opened again.   "It was with their consent of course" I added innocently. She gasped, her eyes wide in horror.   "You, you took the pubic hair samples?".   "Yes, they agreed, it was O.K.".   She was absolutely aghast and admitted later when we told her the truth that she knew that Easterhouse methods were sometimes a little unorthodox, but thought surely even in Easterhouse, you couldn't get away with that.

I was first introduced to Frankie when he leant on

my desk and told me he was under eight so there was
nothing I could do to him.   He continued to be brought
into the office, charged with thefts, housebreakings,
and assaults, but nothing very much happened to him.
One late shift he stood in front of me suspected of hit-
ting an elderly lady with a brick and stealing her purse.
Interviewing him in the presence of his mother, who
had given up all interest in parental control a long time
ago, proved fruitless and they were sent home with the
instruction to report back at the office in the morning,
in the hope that by that time the victim would have provided us with some information.   About an hour later,
a tear stained, dishevelled looking Frankie was pushed
and prodded into the C.I.D. room.   He stood before
us, head bowed.   With prompting in the form of a few
shoves in the back from his brother, he threw a purse on
the table and confessed to the assault and theft.   Ronnie
was no saint and regularly broke into shops and stole
from vans, but he had a strict code of conduct in that
you didn't break into people's houses and you didn't
assault innocent people.   One of his ploys involved his
younger brother, and featured the pedestrian crossing
near their house. When a lorry came along, the younger
boys would cross the road slowly, and while the vehicle
stopped, Ronnie and his pals would relieve the lorry of
part of its load and disappear into the close.   Ronnie had
loosened and cut some floorboards under his bed, which
gave access to a small area of the foundations and it was
there that their spoils were hidden.   Usually the drivers
didn't even realise at the time that a theft had occurred.
I did have a soft spot for Ronnie with his black hair and
very blue eyes and I remember asking him what would

make him give up his life of crime.   He thought about it and shrugged his shoulders "nuthin really".   His girl-friend had given birth to a baby and I congratulated him on being a father and asked what the baby's name was. He immediately turned to his mother "whit's its name ma?".   I was disappointed but not surprised years later when I was told that his morals had slipped and he was involved in the wider aspects of crime.

When I questioned another low life about his life of crime, he explained "<u>You</u> get up early when it's freezing cauld and the rain's peltin doon tae go tae work tae buy things.   Ah get up when ah feel like it an whit ah cannae steal ah kin buy fur hauf the price doon the pub wi ma soshul money".

A fourteen year old boy I had in the office for snatch-ing an old lady's purse was a horrendous little scumbag. So much so, that when his mother called to collect him, I told her what I thought of the foul mouthed, evil, little liar.   Her shoulders sagged and her lip trembled as she explained that he disrupted the household and bullied his brothers and sisters.   She had locks on everything to prevent him stealing.   She had to keep her purse with her at all times.   When she took his clothes away to keep him in, he stole his brother's.   She didn't know what else she could do as she had appealed to the Social Works Department, but the Children's Panel refused to have him put in a home, preferring him to remain within the family and have home calls made.   She couldn't remem-ber the last time he saw a social worker and even then, they were on first name terms and she felt she was the one in the wrong.   Now if she tried to threaten that she would have him put away he laughed at her, "you can't put me away, you've tried". With her permission I put in my report what I thought of this uncontrollable hooligan and recommended that he be detained. Some time later, I met his mother who told me he had been warned about his behaviour and sent home. He was now worse than ever. To endorse my feelings about the effectiveness of the Juvenile Panel, I received a reprimand, asking me to explain on what basis I thought I had the right to call this young boy an inveterate liar!

After a particularly nasty robbery when an Asian man was threatened and assaulted in his general store, Willie and I after a lot of enquiry were successful in apprehending the accused who were later convicted. The shop owner was so grateful that he invited us to his house for a curry. He was most insistent and so one evening, we abandoned our respective spouses and had a beautiful meal with him and his friends. At one point there was great hilarity and it was explained to us that he couldn't make good chapattis and so he had sent out to his local carry-out for them.

There were not many ethnic people living in Easterhouse, perhaps because, although being welcomed by the community in general, their life was made a misery by the local scumbags. One Vietnamese family's house was broken into so many times, they had nothing left to steal. They simply lay in their beds hoping the neds wouldn't attack them. They told their interpreter that living in Easterhouse was worse than crossing the China sea. When they were eventually re-housed, the Torran Toi spray painted the walls claiming a victory.

Apart from assaults, housebreakings were the most common complaint, but even they had their lighter

moments.   When we called at one house, the anxious
woman let us in, and told us to come through, rushing
ahead of us.   When we followed, some steps behind,
we found her at the fish tank.   The neds had taken off
the glass top to feel if there was anything hidden in the
gravel, and she had been instructed by the uniformed
cop not to touch anything in case there were fingerprints. She had spent the whole morning rescuing ener-
getic fish as they made a leap for freedom.

I do believe that some people are evil and J.L.S. was
one of them.   He was 28 years of age when he first came
to our notice.   We were on nightshift when we received
a telephone call from Kirkintilloch Police Office.   A 63
year old woman had been tied up in her home by a man
who broke in.   She was gagged, threatened with a knife
and robbed.   The woman had managed to free herself
and called the police.   While we were interviewing her,
another call was received that a man had broken into a
house.   The couple asleep upstairs heard a noise and
went to investigate.   From the top of the stairs, they saw
some of their personal items in the hall at the front door.
A man then appeared wielding a knife and the couple
barricaded themselves in their bedroom and contacted
the police.   It was obvious from the description that it
was the same man.   As we prepared to go and see them,
a third call came in to say that an adult family of two
brothers and two sisters were grappling with a housebreaker in their bungalow.

It was 3.00 am when the elderly occupants had heard
noises.   They got up to investigate and in the hall
found themselves facing a man brandishing a knife.
Although threatening them, one of the brothers tackled

him.   They knew that their stout wooden outer door was locked and so the two men manhandled him into the space between the doors and locked the glass inner door.   As one of the sisters telephoned the police, J.L.S. smashed his way back into the hall and although one brother received a large gash across his chest and cuts to his head and hand, the family managed to restrain J.L.S. until the arrival of the police.   He was taken to Kirkintilloch Police Office and it was there when typing out the reports, that I had a peculiar, uneasy feeling that sent a shiver through me.   I turned and found the most evil pair of gleaming eyes staring at me from deep sockets.   There was not a movement from him or even a flicker of his eyelids.   I have to confess I have never felt so uncomfortable in anyone's presence either before or since that incident.   I hurriedly finished the paperwork and had him removed to the cells.   We discovered from his criminal record that he had recently been released after serving ten years for rape, assault and robbery.

A few years later I reported for early shift and found the nightshift still busy.   The Detective sergeant told me that he had a friend of mine locked up.   It was J.L.S. Initially it appeared that he had been arrested while attempting to break into a house, but when Eric delved deeper, this depraved pervert proudly divulged that he had followed a young girl home and watched from the rear of the house as her bedroom light illuminated the back garden.   He waited until the house was plunged into darkness and had then made his attempt to break into the house, not as was initially thought, to steal property, but to rape the young occupant.   Eric had the insight to realise that a charge of attempted housebreaking would not reveal J.L.S.'s true intention, and so he charged him with a Breach of the Peace in order to bring out the full circumstances.   J.L.S. received yet another custodial sentence.   This time when I knew he was about due to be released, I contacted the prison service, as I was certain that once he was back on the streets, it would only be a matter of time before he once again committed a serious offence.   He was a time bomb waiting to go off.   Not a question of "if" but "when".   I have to confess I was extremely relieved to discover that this dangerous deviant had committed suicide and was no longer a threat to society.

Even when we knew who was committing house-breakings, it was very difficult to obtain the necessary ingredient to lock them up ... evidence.   In one spate of crimes the method was the same.   Always top flats. One small hole in the ceiling to establish where the bed was, then one larger hole to drop through on to a soft landing.   He never left any fingerprints and would take a taxi straight into the city centre with his ill gotten gains. It was impossible to follow anyone in Easterhouse and it was sheer luck whenever this youth was caught.

One lady whose house had been emptied by house-breakers was furious .... Not at the housebreakers .... Not at the police ....at her dogs!   She had two Easter-house mutts.   When we called at the house we could hear her shouting as she came to the door.   She invited us in and proceeded down the hall.   It was then that we noticed these two small canines with distended stomachs waddling unsteadily ahead of her.   There was a yowl every time she reached them and lashed out with her foot.   As we sat down in the living room, they collapsed at our feet glancing warily at their owner. They visibly cowered as she snarled across at them "bloody dugs. Naebody'll brek intae yer hoose when ye've goat a dug. Oh aye. Bloody wasters. Wee neds emptied the fridge on the flair and these two" .... As her voice got higher, the dogs turned their heads away, moaning softly, their ears flat against their heads. "Ate the lot didn't they. Look at them. Been sick aw morning". We hurriedly concluded our visit and left the unsuccessful guard dogs to their fate.

One dog appeared more conscientious. We had been trying to contact his owner for several days without success, but each time we called and knocked on the door, we could hear this monster setting off down the hall from the living room at the end, his overgrown claws scraping along the linoleum as he screeched to a halt and launched himself at the closed door. Willie pushed open the letter box with his pen but quickly withdrew it as a large set of teeth accompanied by ferocious snarling appeared at the opening. As the noise subsided to a quiet, dangerous growl, Willie stupidly opened the letter box again and grinning like a naughty child, shoved the green crime report through, intending to withdraw it quickly, BUT he wasn't quick enough and was left holding a small ridiculous scrap of paper in his hand as the victorious dog ripped the remainder. When we returned the following day with a photocopy of the report, the owner apologised for his dog's behaviour and handed over the shredded remains of the crime report.

When investigating another housebreaking, we called at the house of a suspect. In answer to our knock, a voice yelled "come in, it's open". We walked down the hall identifying ourselves and the same voice directed us to the bedroom, where we found a couple happily cuddled together in bed. We also immediately spotted a unit with a crack down one side, identical in every way to the one stolen. The suspect burst very quickly "aye, O.K. Duncan sold it to me for £15. Take it away. We don't really like it anyway. It's rubbish".

Another case demonstrated yet again the ned's inability to understand the meaning of "sentimental value". An old lady had been easy prey for a few housebreakers. On this occasion, her T.V., radio and fur coat had been stolen. Willie and I eventually recovered the coat, but were disappointed at not retrieving her T.V. or radio. However her face lit up when she saw her coat "oh, you've got my coat. I knew you'd get it back. You always do". She was absolutely delighted and explained that it had been the last present her husband had bought her before he died suddenly. It was very special to her and for that reason we never told her that we discovered it in a crumpled heap on the floor behind a couch where the occupant of the house described it as "that old rag".

One night as we came into the office we could hear raised voices and loud protestations coming from the uniform bar and went in to investigate. There stood Archie, a well known unsuccessful offender who was constantly in the office for petty offences, his latest scam being the theft of coal from the local hospital. He wore a shabby pair of trousers and a large navy blue pin stripe jacket which hung down unevenly almost to his knees. The padded shoulders extended far beyond Archie's meagre frame and the sleeves obscured his hands. Normally he stood quietly accepting his arrest gracefully, but not that night.   On seeing me he pleaded earnestly.

"Oh Mrs Scott, these two are saying ah wiz stealin coal".

"But Archie, you're always stealing coal".

"Aye but no the night …. Ah mean".

He paused, stepped back and stretched out his arms

"Ah mean, wid ah steal coal wi ma guid jaiket oan".

I took him aside and whispered to him to think of all the times he'd stolen coal and got away with it.   He thought for a few moments and then quietened down.

CHAPTER THIRTY TWO

LEAVING EASTERHOUSE ?

I had been in Easterhouse for a few years when about 5.00 pm one night I received a 'phone call from Cowards Castle.

"This is Headquarters.   Listen carefully, I will not repeat this.   You have to report to the cinema at Pitt Street tomorrow morning at 10.00 am.   Do you understand?"   I confirmed that I did and he then asked to speak to one of my colleagues. I was completely bewildered.   The other officers began to congratulate me, and Ian who had also received the above message.   "I can't be promoted" I protested "I only have one ticket". The police promotion exams were referred to as tickets. There was the Sergeants exam (Elementary) and the Inspectors exam (Advanced).   Although not unheard of, it was more usual for only those possessing both tickets to be promoted.   Each exam in both categories consisted of three papers.   I had failed my advanced ticket by a half mark only to discover that a police officer on the Examinations Board had been handing out the answers to a selected few.   I never sat them again as I wasn't the least ambitious and did not want promotion.

The next morning Ian and I met in the foyer and took our places in the cinema among a very large number of officers.   Perhaps our suspicions should have been aroused then, but they weren't.   An officer in an immaculately pressed uniform and bulled shoes crossed to the dais.   The excited babble of voices hushed immediately.

He adjusted the microphone, cleared his throat and carefully read from a prepared document, "I'm sorry that you were all given such a cryptic message but quite honestly with such short notice we did not have time to explain.   The following officers are to be promoted this morning and I would be obliged if, when your name is called, you proceed to the door (which he indicated), where Sgt. Jones will accompany you to the Chief Constable's Suite.   If the rest of you could remain seated for a few minutes".   He then proceeded to call out the chosen few.   I could sense the tension from Ian on one side of me and the colleague on the other side.   As a name was called, this officer stood up, clenching his fist and whispering softly "yes".   I congratulated him as he left.   Ian sat stiffly as the last name was called.   The officer conducting this shambles waited until the last of the successful group had left and the door closed. Clearing his throat once again and tapping the microphone nervously to ensure that it was still operating efficiently, he continued "I know the rest of you must be disappointed, but I have to tell you that you have all been specially chosen to be part of the newly expanded Serious Crime Squad.   Because of the short notice, if anyone does not want to be part of this Squad, could they make themselves known".   Ian immediately shot out of his seat like a rocket, his refusal coming through clenched teeth, his face mirroring his frustration, anger and disappointment.   I cannot remember if anyone else left, as, unlike Ian, I sat glued to my seat in a trance.   Outside, I met the Detective Chief Inspector who had been in charge of the newly expanded Squad.   He asked me how I felt and I told him I did not want to return.   He assured me that it would be different this time round, but I was not convinced. Back at Easterhouse the story unfolded and my Inspector said he would be sorry to lose me. When I told him I did not want to leave he asked if I meant it and I assured him that I did. He then told me to forget the move, he would deal with it. I heard no more about it, and was delighted when a few months later, Ian got his well deserved promotion.

A lot of time in Easterhouse was taken up attending court which could be quite nerve wracking. One cop could never remember the replies made by the accused. As we sat in the High Court waiting room we decided to teach him the reply in rap ...."I think I must have done it, but I don't remember". As one by one we went in to give our evidence, we left him sitting rehearsing. When his moment came in the witness box we all sat moving our heads in rap time.

Another fellow was caught out when he wrote the reply on the palm of his hand. Unfortunately he was left handed and when he raised his right hand to take the oath, everyone could see his scribbles.

On my numerous visits to courts, my first reply was usually a lie. I had a notice put up on our office board declaring for statement purposes that I was 39 years of age and had 19 years police service. As time went on, the Fiscal would read out "you are Maureen Scott and you are 39 years of age with 19 years police service". I would agree but my fellow officers having given their evidence and sitting in the front row, would very slowly shake their heads. Eventually on my birthdays, they began to scribble the word "still" in front of the 39.

One High Court case was definitely not amusing for

Stevie. We had all given our evidence when the usher called for him. At that point one of the Advocates asked His Lordship if he could be excused for a few moments to visit the toilet. Stevie came in, walked to the witness box, placed his folded fawn raincoat on the seat, stood to attention and raised his hand. "Please sit down" directed the Judge. Stevie looked a little puzzled but sat, placing his hands on his lap, trying hard to give the appearance of being completely relaxed and in control, while a million butterflies fluttered around in his stomach. There was complete silence apart from the occasional distant sound of traffic in Saltmarket and the rustle of papers by the grey wigged, honourable gentlemen seated around a large table in the well of the court. While His Lordship took the opportunity to sip from a glass of water, Stevie stole a glance in our direction to ascertain, as he told us later, that we were all accounted for and no-one had been taken down below for giving some dubious evidence of which he was totally unaware. The minutes passed and he straightened his tie more than once and wiped an imaginary nasal problem with a white handkerchief removed from his folded raincoat. Eventually the Advocate returned, bowed reverently and thanked His Lordship. Proceedings continued, but for Stevie it was the longest few minutes of his life and it was some time after lunch before he fully recovered his composure.

One of the most bizarre cases began one lunchtime with a call from a uniform constable requesting the attendance of the C.I.D. When we arrived at the house, it was complete bedlam. A hysterical woman sat on a couch in the corner of the room being comforted by her husband and re-assured by another man and woman who turned out to be private investigators. In the other corner sat a very subdued, worried little man along with a person who turned out to be his senior partner. Andy, the uniform cop stood between the two opposing sides expressing overwhelming relief on the arrival of the Detective Sergeant and myself. The complicated story began to unfold.

The woman and her husband had been separated and an Interim Interdict was in force. However, recently they had got together again and were trying to resolve their differences. The woman who had a heart complaint and was of a nervous disposition was well known in the G.P. practice to which she belonged. One of the Doctors began calling at the house uninvited and while her husband was at work, bringing her a meal and complimenting her on her appearance. According to the woman, the Doctor told her that due to the Interim Interdict being in force it was forbidden for her husband to enter the house and if he found out that this was the case, he would report the matter to the police. He then used this as a threat to make advances towards her. As the visits and the advances became more frequent and serious, the couple contacted the Samaritans and later private investigators. By this time it had become a usual habit for the Doctor to call on a Tuesday. As the private detective and his assistant sat in the house with the couple, the 'phone rang and the Doctor told the complainer that he was on his way. The husband and the two detectives then hid in the bedroom. A short while later, the accused arrived and he and the complainer went into the living room before making their way to the back bedroom where, after a few minutes, the complainer's raised voice was heard. The husband and two private detectives burst into the bedroom and found the couple lying on the bed, fully clothed but in an intimate embrace. According to the witnesses the shocked accused then apologised and admitted that he had been foolish. The police were sent for and the doctor's senior partner. During this chaos, the poor woman collapsed and as it was feared she may have suffered a heart attack, the accused attended to her, but this proved unsatisfactory for as she came to and saw him bending over her she became hysterical. An ambulance was summoned and she was removed to hospital.

A few months later at the trial, it was revealed that the doctor had been under a considerable amount of pressure and Mr. Beltrami, defending well, produced a surprise witness who testified that the complainer was prone to exaggeration. The accused was found ..... Not Guilty!

As in the police, the courts had Sheriffs who were real characters. The favourite was Irvine Smith. It was a well known fact that a ned would alter his plea to not guilty if he found he was appearing before him in the hope that on his next appearance he would appear before the Sheriff commonly known as Santa Claus for obvious reasons. Mr. Smith had the most wonderful wit and was never moved or fooled by a lawyer's attempt to "canonise" his client. For example, as one lawyer expounded "my client is a Jekyll and Hyde character" he was interrupted by Mr. Smith "In that case then, I find Dr. Jekyll not guilty, but Mr. Hyde guilty and I sentence him to two years imprisonment".

One man appearing in his Court was told "your behaviour was disgraceful and disgusting. I sentence you to two years imprisonment". The accused did not quite hear his sentence and asked the policeman by his side who told him "he says you're a dirty old man and sentenced you to three years". Irvine Smith interrupted "Constable, I don't mind you paraphrasing my English, but I must object to you increasing my sentence".

In Easterhouse we had every cause to be grateful to him. When one of our uniform cops sadly died after a long illness, our local neds appearing at court were jubilant, smirking that their cases wouldn't go ahead because there was now only one witness. They were all intending pleading not guilty. However they reckoned without Irvine Smith who saw no reason why the cases shouldn't go ahead with one witness and sufficient evidence. The word soon reached the ears of our scumbags.

Identification Parades were common place but very time consuming. For something fairly trivial or where there was no fear of intimidation, they were held at the office, but more and more they were conducted at Divisional Headquarters where a proper identification unit was constructed with one-way glass and witness rooms for before and after the viewing. The Easterhouse parades had their humorous moments. They were also a source of income for the clientele of the nearby pub who took their part as stand ins very seriously. At Baird Street, the local men's hostel was a popular venue for stand ins, and it was quite difficult to convince a well lived in face of 60 years, that he was not suitable as a stand in for a 20 year old suspect.

One man suspected of a fraud greeted the witness with

a friendly smile "oh hullo, it's you again".

Another suspect called at the office with a black eye. I made a quick visit to the shopping centre and bought some cheap make up. The suspect and his lawyer were quite impressed with my handiwork on the stand ins.

More serious was the parade at Baird Street of a man suspected of committing a robbery in which a shotgun had been used. One of the witnesses asked that the group say the words "hand over the money". As all the stand ins did as requested, they raised their hand as though they were holding a gun, except the suspect who raised both hands as one would hold a shotgun.

CHAPTER THIRTY THREE

LEAVING EASTERHOUSE

After seven hard but most enjoyable years in Easterhouse, meeting the best and the worst people, I suddenly began to feel a bit tired.   The uncertainty of each day had lost its excitement.   A few of my colleagues had moved on to other things, and I began to feel ready for a change.   I applied for something completely different …. A C.I.D. posting at Glasgow Airport, and was delighted but also a little sad when I was told my application had been successful.   On my last day I put up the statutory bottle of whisky, and felt quite emotional as one of the detective Sergeants gave a little speech and presented me with a gold pen from the boys.   The seriousness of the moment was interrupted by a knock at the door and a uniform cop spotted me "Maureen, we've got a body for the theft of the prescription pad from the doctor's surgery.   It's your case.   He's been passing them in chemists all over the city …. Another Easterhouse saga ….but not mine anymore.

My final visit to Easterhouse Police Office came some months later.   Besides my other duties at Glasgow Airport, I was stationery officer.   I could order anything I wanted.   As Christmas approached, I got a large cardboard box and painted a red cross on it.   I then filled it with box files, pens, pencils, staples, white out, not forgetting paper clips and all sorts of other goodies seldom seen at Easterhouse, and delivered it with a note "A Red Cross parcel" from Maureen.

The work at Glasgow Airport was completely different, and it was nice to meet happy holiday makers and travellers, but after almost two years I received another summons. I was being transferred to Headquarters. I became a Cowards Castle employee, where I discovered that, although I was no longer involved in the sagas of Easterhouse, hard work comes in various forms.

In 1993, after thirty years of the happiest and saddest times of my life, I retired. As the cop said on my first nightshift … T.J.F. …. But it's still the only job I would have chosen.

JE NE REGRETTE RIEN

THE END